GAMSAT PREPARATION B
PRACTICE QUESTIONS
for Section I

By Dr Peter Griffiths BA (Hons) MBBS MSc

For our full range of Gamsat preparation materials please visit the website at www.gamsatreview.com

Published by Dr Peter Griffiths

Copyright © Peter J Griffiths 2019

First published 2019

ISBN-13: 9781795422741

All rights reserved. No part of this publication may be translated or reproduced, stored in a retrieval system, or transmitted in any form or by any means, electronic, mechanical, photocopying, recording or otherwise, without the prior permission of the publisher.

The use in this publication of trade names, trademarks, service marks, and similar terms even if they are identified as such, is not to be taken as an expression of opinion as to whether or not they are subject to proprietary rights.

While every care has been taken to ensure that the information in this book is correct at the time of publication no guarantee or warranty express or implied is made with respect to the material contained herein. Neither the author nor the publisher can accept any legal responsibility for any errors or omissions that may be made or for any loss or damage caused by reliance on the information contained herein.

The right of Peter J Griffiths to be identified as the author of this work has been asserted by him in accordance with the Copyright Designs and Patents Act 1988.

Permissions may be sought from peter@gamsatreview.com

www.gamsatreview.com

Table of Contents

Introduction 1

Questions Unit 1 2

Solutions to Practice Questions ANSWERS 44

Introduction

Thank you for purchasing this book, here is your FREE BONUS

Get more FREE PRACTICE QUESTIONS at

www.gamsatreview.com/gamsat-practice-questions

Just scroll to the bottom of the page for the link

Please also visit the main website to see all our Gamsat preparation material including the best selling Griffiths Gamsat Review which has helped thousands of students pass Gamsat since 2005.

www.gamsatreview.com

You can also follow us on Instagram & Twitter for updates & advice about the test @GamsatReview

Questions Unit 1
Questions 1-5

The passage below is taken from the essay *Mysticism and logic* in which Bertrand Russell defines insight and mystic illumination.

Passage 1

Questions 1 & 2

There is, first, the belief in insight as against discursive analytic knowledge: the belief in a way of wisdom, sudden, penetrating, coercive, which is contrasted with the slow and fallible study of outward appearance by a science relying wholly upon the senses. All who are capable of absorption in an inward passion must have experienced at times the strange feeling of unreality in common objects, the loss of contact with daily things, in which the solidity of the outer world is lost, and the soul seems, in utter loneliness, to bring forth, out of its own depths, the mad dance of fantastic phantoms which have hitherto appeared as independently real and living. This is the negative side of the mystic's initiation: the doubt concerning common knowledge, preparing the way for the reception of what seems a higher wisdom. Many men to whom this negative experience is familiar do not pass beyond it, but for the mystic it is merely the gateway to an ampler world.

The first and most direct outcome of the moment of illumination is belief in the possibility of a way of knowledge which may be called revelation or insight or intuition, as contrasted with sense, reason, and analysis, which are regarded as blind guides leading to the morass of illusion. Closely connected with this belief is the conception of a Reality behind the world of appearance and utterly different from it. This Reality is regarded with an admiration often amounting to worship; it is felt to be always and everywhere close at hand, thinly veiled by the shows of sense, ready, for the receptive mind, to shine in its glory even through the apparent folly and wickedness of man.

The poet, the artist, and the lover are seekers after that glory: the haunting beauty that they pursue is the faint reflection of its sun. But the mystic lives in the full light of the vision: what others dimly seek he knows, with a knowledge beside which all other knowledge is ignorance.

1 Which of the following statements best sums up the difference between discursive and coercive knowledge?

A Discursive knowledge relies on scientific observation, while coercive knowledge relies on the senses.
B Discursive knowledge relies on the senses, while coercive knowledge is extra-sensory.
C Discursive knowledge is the quickest route to genuine knowledge, while coercive insights negate such knowledge.
D Discursive knowledge is based on insight, while coercive knowledge is based on intuition.

2 As regards the accurate apprehension of reality, the author makes clear that

A reality can only be apprehended through intuitive illumination, not through science.
B only mystics have a true apprehension and understanding of reality.
C the visionary world of the mystic is a reflection of the empirical world we live in.
D the illusionary reality of the mystic is preferable to discursive reality.

Passage 2

Questions 3 & 4

The second characteristic of mysticism is its belief in unity, and its refusal to admit opposition or division anywhere. We found Heraclitus saying "good and ill are one"; and again he says, "the way up and the way down is one and the same." The same attitude appears in the simultaneous assertion of contradictory propositions, such as: "We step and do not step into the same rivers; we are and are not." The assertion of Parmenides, that reality is one and indivisible, comes from the same impulse towards unity.

A third mark of almost all mystical metaphysics is the denial of the reality of Time. This is an outcome of the denial of division; if all is one, the distinction of past and future must be illusory. We have seen this doctrine prominent in Parmenides; and among moderns it is fundamental in the systems of Spinoza and Hegel.

Four questions thus arise in considering the truth or falsehood of mysticism, namely:

 I. Are there two ways of knowing, which may be called respectively reason and intuition? And if so, is either to be preferred to the other?

 II. Is all plurality and division illusory?

 III. Is time unreal?

 IV. What kind of reality belongs to good and evil?

On all four of these questions, while fully developed mysticism seems to me mistaken, I yet believe that, by sufficient restraint, there is an element of wisdom to be learned from the mystical way of feeling, which does not seem to be attainable in any other manner. If this is the truth, mysticism is to be commended as an attitude towards life, not as a creed about the world. The meta-physical creed, I shall maintain, is a mistaken outcome of the emotion, although this emotion, as colouring and informing all other thoughts and feelings, is the inspirer of whatever is best in mankind. Even the cautious and patient investigation of truth by science, which seems the very antithesis of the mystic's swift certainty, may be fostered and nourished by that very spirit of reverence in which mysticism lives and moves.

3   The mystic apprehension of time is the outcome of the mystic's perception that there is a

A   lack of a universal division or opposition.
B   disparity of human experience over time.
C   dichotomy between reason and intuition.
D   plurality of good and evil.

4   In summing up his views in the final paragraph, the author makes clear that.

A   he is a mystic who is sympathetic to reason.
B   he is a rationalist who rejects mystic impulses.
C   mysticism is a mistaken response to reality.
D   he is a rationalist who is sympathetic to intuition.

Unit 2

Questions 5-7

The passage below looks at progress, and the lack thereof, in regards to putting genetically modified, farm-raised salmon on the market.

After 18 years spent leaping over regulatory hurdles and sputtering in political gridlock, the first genetically modified animal intended for human consumption is one critical step closer to receiving federal approval.

Although consumers are wary of genetically modified food, and government reportedly ran unprecedented interference, independent biologists, geneticists and environmentalists — including the Veterinary Medicine Advisory Committee (VMAC) appointed by the Food and Drug Administration to review the application — found the enhanced salmon entirely safe. The AquAdvantage salmon combines two key pieces of DNA from the Chinook salmon and a fish called the Ocean Pout with the Atlantic salmon. This allows the altered salmon to grow to market size in about half the time.

Some experts argue the Massachusetts company in question, AquaBounty Technologies, represents the very best about the use of biotechnology in food application, and what's become the very worst — the regulatory holdups.

"We have to take advantage of every technology," says geneticist Dr. Mark Walton, who began the non-profit *Feed the Real World* after years as a biotechnology industry CEO due to his frustration with misrepresentations about food production. "The travesty is that the process has been subverted by commercial and political interests."

AquaBounty approached the FDA with its initial application 18 years ago. In 2010, the FDA and its advisory committee of experts had a final hearing to evaluate the data. According to Alison Van Eenennaam, an animal biotechnology expert from VMAC, the fish went through the "an extensive federal regulatory review," which shows safety for consumption and has minimal environmental risk.

"The FDA and VMAC agreed the data presented showed no difference between this fish and a conventional Atlantic salmon with regard to food safety," said Van Eenennaam. "And the environmental concerns have been largely mitigated through the proposed conditions of use in land-based facilities with multiple redundant containment approaches to prevent release."

AquAdvantage salmon is sustainably farmed using land-based tank facilities with multiple containment measures. Although the FDA declared "no significant impact" in the environmental assessment, the application still sat in limbo. If there's no more political undermining, the FDA will review public feedback to the assessment released just last year.

"There's nothing in this fish that gives us any indication there's a problem to the food supply," says molecular geneticist and food safety expert Alan McHughen.

5   Based on the passage we can safely infer that

A   the government is cautiously supportive of genetically modified animals.
B   the government is determined to keep genetically modified animals off the market.
C   the author believes the benefits of genetically modified food outweigh the risks.
D   the author is biased against government regulation of genetically modified meats.

6   AquaBounty Technologies CEO Dr. Mark Walton

A   is motivated to develop better salmon by the desire to alleviate global hunger.
B   welcomes scientific scrutiny of his company's genetically modified salmon.
C   believes his government is not acting in the best interests of consumers.
D   feels that government has no viable role in the regulation of the biotechnology industry.

7   Based on the article, which of the following factors poses the only legitimate concern associated with the mass production of genetically modified salmon?

A   The scientific community is generally wary of genetically modified foods.
B   Governmental regulatory agencies lack the technology to properly assess risks associated with genetically modified animals.
C   Federal regulatory review shows that genetically modified fish pose minimal environmental risk.
D   Genetically modified salmon will undermine more traditional methods of procuring live salmon.

Unit 3

Questions 8-10

The passage below from African Trader by W. H Kingston considers different factors affecting mortality rates amongst African slaves held in port and during passage from Africa to the Caribbean and the Americas in the late 18th century. The diagram that follows, gives relevant data showing mortality rates in port and during the passage, 1790-1800. Consider the passage and table to answer the questions that follow.

African slaves were harvested from large catchment areas, each with its own demographic along the coast and within the African interior, thus accounting for a wide diversity of origins and ethnicities on any given voyage. Cargo ships, however, left Africa through very few ports of embarkation. The trade from each of these ports had its own character and profile, and different ports tended to supply slaves to the same destinations over time. Gambia, for example, catered to the Portuguese, providing nearly 90% of all slaves exported to Brazil, while 7 of every 10 slaves reaching the American colonies derived from Bight of Benin or Congo/Angola. Cuba, on the other hand, represents the opposite extreme, receiving more than 50% of all slaves exported, but receiving no more than 10% of its slave population from any given port. Slaves were likely exposed to new diseases, malnutrition and starvation not only on board ship, but during forced marches from their areas of origin, in detainment camps while awaiting boarding, and in ship's holds prior to ever leaving port.

The trans-Atlantic crossing of slaves from Africa to the Caribbean and the Americas was long and arduous, with an average of 13% of slaves dying while being held as cargo in port and/or during transport. Experienced shipmasters who were able to deliver their cargo (slaves) alive were in high demand, and the Doughtry Act allowed for a £50 bonus per passage for those shipmasters whose vessels had a mortality rate below 3%. Shipmasters desirous of securing the bonus noted that a variety of factors could potentially affect mortality rates, and the most successful masters knew how to pick their passages.

The chart below that gives data on the trans-Atlantic slave trade from 1790 to 1800:

Diagram I

Country of Origin	# of Passages	# of days in port	# of days spent in passage	Percentage of Male Slaves	Percent of fatalities in port	Percent of fatalities during passage
Congo-Angola	67	86	66	55	8.2	4.9
Windward Coast	19	75	68	65	3.5	2.7
Gambia	50	71	65	68	3.1	2.2
Sierra Leone	107	58	75	65	3.7	2.5
Gold Coast	30	99	80		2.7	2.0
Bight of Biafra	111	120	75	56	10.6	11.7
Senegambia	6	176	29	66	1.2	1.7

8   Based on the passage we can safely infer that

A   more slaves were transported to Brazil than to any other destination.
B   the Cuban slave population was ethnically more diverse than slave populations in other destinations.
C   shipmasters were able to take concrete steps to reduce slave mortality rates during the passage.
D   no shipmasters received the Doughtry bonus as over 3% of all slaves died in port or during the passage.

9   The data provided in the table suggests that shipmasters wishing to improve their odds of earning the £50 should pay special attention to the

A   duration of the passage.
B   male to female ratio amongst slaves.
C   number of overall passages made.
D   number of days the spent in port.

10 Consider the statements below in the context of the data presented and answer the question that follows.

I   More slaves died in port than during the trans-Atlantic crossing.

II Some passages are statistically bound to have higher mortality rates than others.

III Female slaves from Senegambia balanced the disparity between males and females coming from other countries.

IV The majority of humans transported as cargo to the Caribbean and the Americas came from Bight of Biafra.

V   Women were likely more prone to dying in port or in passage than men.

Which of the statements above is supported by the data provided in the graph?

A   Statements I, II, and III
B   Statements II, II, I and V
C   *Statements I, II and V.*
D   Statements II, I, IV and V.

Unit 4

Questions 11 - 15

Authors Louise and Ralph Benedict propose that we can easily determine an individual's character based on their physical appearance.

Questions 11 & 12

Whether you are a blade of grass on the Nevada desert or a man in the streets of London, you can win only as you adapt yourself to your environment. Today our environmental problem consists largely of the other fellow.

To adapt to the contemporary environment, it is necessary to better understand our neighbours—to recognize that people differ from each other in their likes and dislikes, traits, talents, tendencies and capabilities. The combination of these makes each individual's nature. It is not difficult to understand others for with each group of these traits there always goes its corresponding physical makeup--the externals whereby the internal is invariably indicated. This is true of every species on the globe and of every subdivision within each species.

All dogs belong to the same species but there is a great difference between the "nature" of a St. Bernard and that of a terrier, just as there is a decided difference between the natures of different human beings. But in both instances the actions, reactions and habits of each can be accurately anticipated on sight by the shape, size and structure of the two creatures.

When a terrier comes into the room you instinctively draw away unless you want to be jumped at and greeted effusively. But you make no such movement to protect yourself from a St. Bernard because you read, on sight, the different natures of these two from their external appearance.

Goaded by the instinct of self-preservation, man, like all other living things, has made heroic efforts to meet the demands of his environment. He has been more successful than any other creature and is, as a result, the most complex organism on the earth. But his most baffling complexities resolve themselves into comparatively simple terms once it is recognized that each internal change brought about by his environment brought with it the corresponding external mechanism without which he could not have survived.

11   Consider each of the statements below to determine which is not supported by the passage.

A   Humans are becoming more socially adept.
B   Personality dictates body type.
C   Body type indicates behaviour.
D   People from a remote village will look and act similarly.

12   Which of the terms below best describes the author's perception of man?

A   ethnocentric
B   anthropocentric
C   xenophobic
D   anthropoidal

Passage 2

Questions 13 - 15

Learning to read people is also a simpler process than learning to read books because there are fewer letters in the human alphabet. Though man seems to the untrained eye a mystifying mass of "funny little marks," he is not now difficult to analyze. All physical characteristics emanate from our most basic instincts: fear, hunger, anxiety, hope, etc. and find their expression in the face and physique of the individual.

The larger any part or organ the better its equipment for carrying out the work of that organ and the more does it tend to express itself. Nature IS an efficiency expert and doesn't give you an oversupply of anything without demanding that you use it.

Our ancestors developed massive jaws as a result of constant combat. As fast as civilization decreased the necessity for combat Nature decreased the size of the average human jaw. But wherever you see a large protruding jaw you see an individual 'armed and engined,' as Kipling says, for some kind of fighting. The large jaw always goes with a combative nature, whether it is found on a man or a woman, a child, a pugilist or a minister.

Let us consider, for a moment, our pugilistic friends the Irish. As the inheritance of a fighting ancestor it is the result of millions of years of fighting in prehistoric times, and, like any other over-developed part or organ, it has an intense urge to express itself. This inherent urge is what makes the owner of that jaw "fight at the drop of the hat," and often have "a chip on his shoulder."

Thus, because every external characteristic is the result of natural laws, and chiefly of natural selection, the vital traits of any creature can be read from his externals. Every student of biology, anatomy, anthropology, ethnology or psychology is familiar with these facts.

13 Which of the following slogans, if true, would be consistent with the authors' views?

A   You can't judge a book by its cover.
B   It's never too late to change.
C   Appearances are deceiving.
D   Seeing is believing.

14 A prominent jaw in a modern person is not a

A   result of fighting.
B   cause of anti-social behaviour.
C   result of a pugilistic personality
D   result of ancestry.

15 Consider the table below and answer the question that follows.

Ad populum maintains a proposition to be true on the grounds that many or most people believe it.	**False Analogy** reaches a conclusion based on a faulty comparison.
Cherry picking occurs when only that data favourable to the proposition is used in the course of the argument.	**Association fallacy** maintains that the qualities of one thing are inherently qualities of another, by making an irrelevant association.

Which of the logic fallacies described above does not deter the author's argument that physical characteristics derive from environmental exigency and pre-determine human behaviour and that such behaviours and characteristics change when the environment changes?

A   ad populum
B   defective induction
C   cherry picking
D   association fallacy

Unit 5:

Questions 16-21

In the passage below, adapted from Clarice Lispector's short story *The smallest woman in the world*, man of the world and explorer Marcel Pretre meets Little Flower, the smallest woman in the world, whom he discovers in the depths of equatorial Africa.

Passage 1

Questions 16-18

In the depths of Equatorial Africa the French explorer, Marcel Pretre, hunter and man of the world, came across a tribe of surprisingly small pygmies. Therefore he was even more surprised when he was informed that a still smaller people existed, beyond forests and distances. So he plunged farther on.

That was the way, then, that the explorer discovered, standing at his very feet, the smallest existing human thing. His heart beat, because no emerald in the world is so rare. The teachings of the wise men of India are not so rare. The richest man in the world has never set eyes on such a strange grace. Right there was a woman that the greed of the most exquisite dream could never have imagined. It was then that the explorer said timidly, and with a delicacy of feeling of which his wife would never have thought him capable: "You are Little Flower."

So there she stood, the smallest woman in the world. For an instant, in the buzzing heat, it seemed as if the Frenchman had unexpectedly reached his final destination. Probably only because he was not insane, his soul neither wavered nor broke its bounds. Feeling an immediate necessity for order and for giving names to what exists, he called her Little Flower. And in order to be able to classify her among the recognizable realities, he immediately began to collect facts about her.

At that moment, Little Flower scratched herself where no one scratches. The explorer—as if he were receiving the highest prize for chastity to which an idealistic man dares aspire—the explorer, experienced as he was, looked the other way.

A photograph of Little Flower was published in the coloured supplement of the Sunday Papers, life-size. She was wrapped in cloth, her belly already very big. The flat nose, the black face, the splay feet. She looked like a dog.

On that Sunday, in an apartment, a woman seeing the picture of Little Flower in the paper didn't want to look a second time because "It gives me the creeps."

16   As a statement on colonial exploration the author makes clear that she

A   condones colonial exploitation of natural resources including humans for their own good.
B   she condemns the actions of the French explorer and the people he represents.
C   aims merely to depict the relationship between colonialists and the people they colonize.
D   she is sympathetic to the needs of both the colonialist and the colonized.

17   Pretre's fascination with Little Flower stems from his

A   commitment to his profession.
B   tendency to objectify her.
C   genuine admiration of her beauty.
D   fascination with her tiny size.

18   Which statement below best characterizes the relationship between Petre and Little Flower as depicted in the passage above?

A   Theirs is a symbiotic relationship.
B   The relationship is mutually exploitative.
C   The relationship is a case of mutual infatuation.
D   The relationship is a figment of Pretre's imagination.

Passage 2

Questions 19-21

In the meanwhile, in Africa, the explorer studied that little belly of the smallest mature human being. It was at this moment that the explorer, for the first time since he had known her, instead of feeling curiosity, or exaltation, or victory, or the scientific spirit, felt sick.

The smallest woman in the world had started to laugh.

She was laughing, warm, warm—Little Flower was enjoying life. The rare thing herself was experiencing the ineffable sensation of not having been eaten yet. Not having been eaten yet was something that at any other time would have given her the agile impulse to jump from branch to branch. But, in this moment of tranquillity, amid the thick leaves of the Eastern Congo, she was not putting this impulse into action—it was entirely concentrated in the smallness of the rare thing itself. So she was laughing. It was a laugh such as only one who does not speak laughs. It was a laugh that the explorer, constrained, couldn't classify. And she kept on enjoying her own soft laugh, she who wasn't being devoured. Not to be devoured is the most perfect feeling. Not to be devoured is the secret goal of a whole life. While she was not being eaten, her bestial laughter was as delicate as joy is delicate. The explorer was baffled.

The rare thing herself felt in her breast a warmth that might be called love. She loved that sallow explorer. If she could have talked and had told him that she loved him, he would have been puffed up with vanity - vanity that would have collapsed when she added that she also loved the explorer's ring very much, and the explorer's boots. And when that collapse had taken place, Little Flower would not have understood why. Because her love for the explorer—one might even say "profound love," since, having no other resources, she was reduced to a profundity— her profound love for the explorer would not have been at all diminished by the fact that she also loved his boots. Little Flower blinked with love, and laughed warmly, small, gravid, warm.

19   What prompts Pretre to feel sick?

A   He realizes Little Flower loves her life.
B   He fears Little Flower will die in labour.
C   He realizes he loves Little Flower
D   He realizes Little Flower loves him.

20   What prompts Little Flower to laugh?

A   her eminent delivery
B   unembellished existence
C   her dreams of a better life
D   her love for the explorer

21   Little Flower's love for the explorer would best be characterized as

A   unconditional love.
B   conditional love.
C   perverse love.
D   unrequited love.

Unit 6

Questions 22 & 23

The passage below explores the hold ups with embryonic stem cell treatments and alternative options for Americans who cannot receive such treatments in the US. The graph that follows provides information from an attitudinal survey of church members regarding the morality of stem cell research.

To the majority of the people in the US, "stem cells" mean "embryonic stem cells" - the cells which scientists need to destroy an embryo to obtain. Embryonic stem cell research gets attention, but embryonic stem cells have not treated a single patient.

While American stem cell research remains obsessed with embryos and mired in politics, in other countries; several Asian countries, Mexico, Germany, Argentina, Peru, Switzerland and the U.K. - adult stem cells have helped patients with everything from diabetes to Parkinson's disease.

Adult stem cells can be found in every person's skin, bone marrow, brain, blood vessels, skeletal muscles and liver. Medical teams can remove adult stem cells from patients, then multiply the stem cells in laboratories. When the stem cells are reintroduced into patients, they help grow new, healthy tissue.

What are the implications of this technology? Parkinson's patients can receive stem cells that produce dopamine, helping to reverse the effects of their disease. Heart disease patients can reverse cardiovascular damage using their own stem cells.

Numerous patients, with over 100 'incurable' diseases, have significantly improved their health through adult stem cell technology and can now enjoy a better quality of life. Adult stem cells have helped patients with cancers, liver failure, autoimmune diseases, spinal cord injury -; even broken bones and infected surface wounds.

Thousands of Americans are dying needlessly each month. I founded the International Centre for Adult Stem Cell Education (ICASCE) to educate the American public on the potential of adult stem cells for diagnosing, treating, curing and preventing disease.

Americans should not suffer and die without knowing that adult stem cells exist. Americans can receive immediate, life-changing treatments for Hodgkin's Lymphoma, sickle cell anaemia, multiple sclerosis, breast cancer and many other diseases -; if they look outside of America.

Data pertaining to the moral acceptability of stem cell research by church attendance sheds some light on the matter:

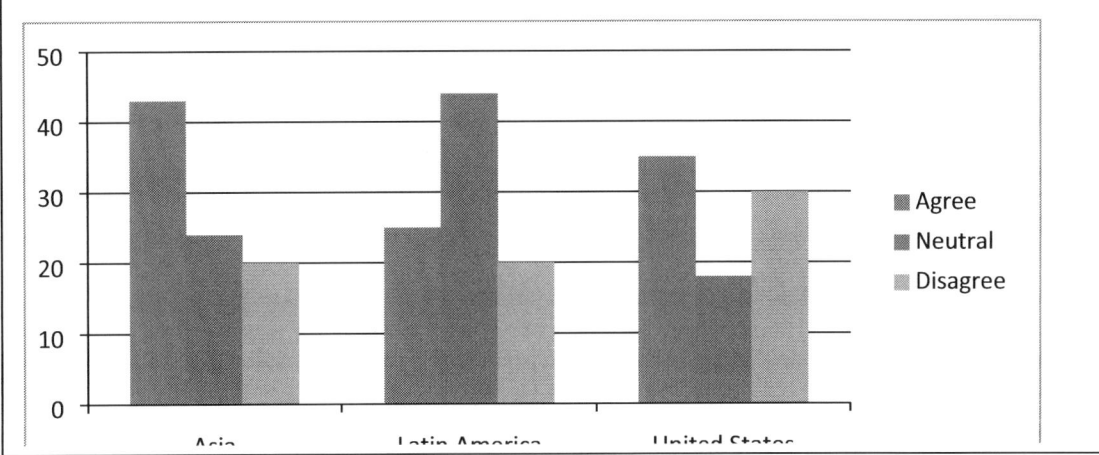

Moral Acceptability of Stem Cell Research by Church Attendance

Question: Regardless of whether or not it is legal, please indicate if you feel stem cell research is morally acceptable (agree), if you have no opinion or are undecided about stem cell research (neutral) or if you feel it is morally unacceptable (disagree).

22 Consider the statements below to determine which sums up the status of stem cell research in the US compared to the other countries mentioned in the article.

A US policy on embryonic stem cell research is likely the same as that of the other countries mentioned in the article.
B US policy on embryonic stem cell research likely differs from that of the other countries mentioned in the article.
C US politicians are likely heavily influenced by conservative religious groups who oppose harvesting human embryos.
D US policy on stem cell research is likely influenced by the fact that US scientists are heavily invested in embryonic stem cell research.

23 Taken together, the passage and data provided in the graph suggest that churchgoers are

A the reason stem cell research is on hold in the US.
B mostly in favor of stem cell research.
C mostly against stem cell research.
D mostly undecided about stem cell research.

Unit 7

Questions 24 - 30

Governments around the world are considering lifetime post-custodial civil commitment as an add-on to prison sentences for sex offenders. The passage below explains civil commitment, while the diagram that follows provides data pertaining to victims and their relationship to their perpetrators. Analyze both and answer the questions that follow.

Passage 1

Questions 24 & 25

Governments are getting tough on sex offenders, adopting residency restrictions that essentially shut convicted offenders out of entire cities. National TV personalities have launched a concerted effort to rid communities of "predators." Several states are considering joining the 16 with civil commitment statutes that allow them to keep sex offenders in state custody--usually in secure facilities operated by state mental health or human services agencies--after they have completed sentences for their crimes.

But it is not just lawmakers and everyday citizens who are concerned. In several states, a chorus of offender treatment professionals, victim services providers, mental health advocates, and in some cases even law enforcement and corrections professionals believes that the policy discussion's tone is furthering misconceptions about who sex offenders are and whether they ultimately can be housed safely in the community. And they say the misinformation that's out there actually can serve to make communities less safe, by diverting attention from a hidden majority of offenders.

"We need the public and policy makers to understand that offenders are not all the same," says Anne Liske, executive director of the New York State Coalition Against Sexual Assault. New York legislators this year discussed but did not adopt a potentially broad and expensive measure for civil commitment of sex offenders upon sentence completion. Liske terms such a strategy as "a solution that addresses a small portion of the population with a huge allocation of resources."

24   Underlying the public's outcry for post-custodial civil commitment is the premise that

A   the law applies equally to all.
B   prevention is better than cure.
C   only some sex offenders can be rehabilitated.
D   communities cannot be kept safe from sex offenders.

25   Those engaged most directly with the perpetrators and victims of sex crimes are concerned about the passage of civil commitment statutes because

A   the proposed legislation ignores the fact that most sex offenders can be rehabilitated.
B   the proposed legislation is prejudicial to sex offenders.
C   the proposed legislation will make communities less safe.
D   civil commitment amounts to an automatic life-sentence regardless of the circumstances.

Passage 2

Questions 26-30

Indeed, the term "sex offender" applies to a broad range of individuals in most states, and the parameters vary from state to state. In Ohio, for example, the crimes that fall under the umbrella of sex offenses encompass four separate categories in the law. These categories of crime include violent offenses such as rape and the sexual assault of a child; they also include illegal use of a minor for sexual activity, menacing/stalking activity that is conducted with a sexual motivation, and crimes such as kidnapping if it is committed with a sexual motivation.

While the public and media's attention is transfixed on the stranger who invades a community, the more typical profile of a sex offender is the relative, family friend, or other meaningful person in a victim's life, many advocates say. Yet they say strategies such as civil commitment tend to consider all offenders as having the characteristics of the habitual child predator, ignoring data showing that most sex offenders are less likely to commit repeat offenses than other categories of felons.

These advocates are careful not to minimize the dangers that the "worst of the worst" offenders pose, and acknowledge that for these individuals a treatment-focused, community-based approach is virtually certain to fail. But many say that when they try to highlight the progress that can be made through treatment for the vast majority of offenders, they too feel under siege.

"People who say that something can be done end up getting attacked," says David D'Amora, who runs the Centre for the Treatment of Problem Sexual Behaviour in Connecticut. "As treatment professionals, we end up becoming suspect, so we find that we need to connect with victim services, police, and other groups to get the message out."

The graphic below categorizes sex offenders based on their relationship to the victim:

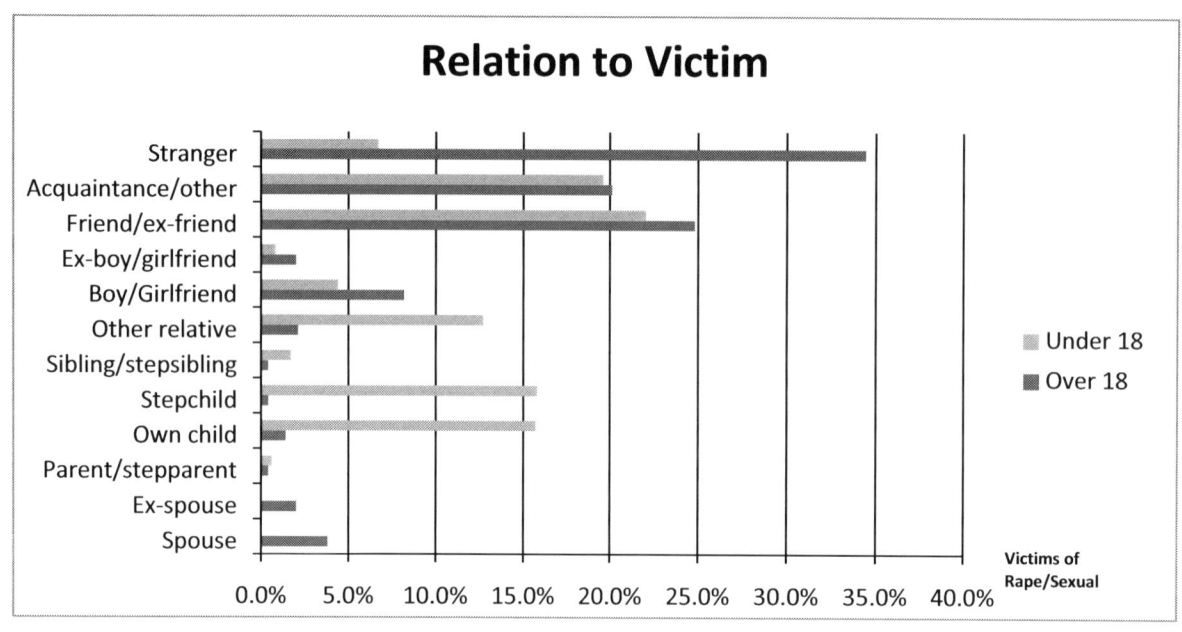

26 The author includes a listing of the broad categories of sex offenders to convince readers that

A not all categories of sex offences are heinous and merit custodial care.
B sex offense crimes stem primarily from mental health issues.
C sex crimes have as yet to be adequately defined.
D he sympathizes with the public's call for legislation to protect communities.

27 An underlying flaw in the reasoning behind civil commitment is that

A recidivism rates are higher amongst sex offenders than amongst other ex-felons.
B recidivism rates are lower amongst sex offenders than amongst other ex-felons.
C there is no mechanism for determining which sex offender might and who might not reoffend.
D those with the most expertise are attacked for their opinions regardless of what the data says.

28 D'Amora's statement that treatment professionals need to connect with victim, legal and other groups suggests that

A these groups are in favour of the proposed civil care legislation.
B these are the groups that attack treatment professionals.
C these groups have not been adequately consulted about the proposed legislation.
D these groups oppose the proposed civil care legislation.

29   Based on the aims of the proposed civil care legislation as described in the passage and the data presented in the graph, we can safely say that as proposed, civil care legislation will likely

A   protect the majority of children from sexual offenses.
B   protect neither victims not communities from sexual predators
C   prevent only a minority of sexual offenses against children from occurring.
D   prevent the majority of sexual offenses against adults from occurring.

30   Based on the data presented in the graphic, we can develop a profile of the typical or most common victim of sexual offenses. He or she is most likely to be:

A   under 18 and victimized by a parent or stepparent.
B   18 or older and victimized by a stranger.
C   under 18 and victimized by a non-relative.
D   18 or older and victimized by a friend or former friend.

Unit 8

Questions 31 & 32

Cartoons rely on verbal and non-verbal clues to convey their meaning. Analyze the cartoon below and answer the questions that follow.

31 The cartoon implies that

A   God is an uncaring, not a beneficent, being.
B   there is no God to answer our prayers.
C   our prayers are heard but go unanswered.
D   praying to God is a futile endeavour.

32 If the young man pictured represents mankind, we can say that man is

A   malleable.
B   fatuous.
C   ingénue.
D   trenchant.

Unit 9

Questions 33-37

Veterinarian R.A. Craig differentiates between illnesses and diseases and between infectious and contagious diseases in the passage below.

Passage 1

Questions 33 & 34

Disease is the general term for any deviation from the normal or healthy condition of the body. The morbid processes that result in either slight or marked modifications of the normal condition are recognized by the injurious changes in the structure or function of the organ, or group of body organs involved. The increase in the secretion of urine noticeable in horses in the late fall and winter is caused by the cool weather and the decrease in the perspiration. If, however, the increase in the quantity of urine secreted occurs independently of any normal cause and is accompanied by an unthrifty and weakened condition of the animal, it would then characterize disease. Tissues may undergo changes in order to adapt themselves to different environments, or as a means of protecting themselves against injuries. The coat of a horse becomes heavy and appears rough if the animal is exposed to severe cold. A rough, staring coat is very common in horses affected by disease. The outer layer of the skin becomes thickened when subject to pressure or friction from the harness. This change in structure is purely protective and normal. In disease the deviation from normal must be more permanent in character than it is in the examples mentioned above, and in some way prove injurious to the body functions.

We may divide diseases into three classes: non-specific, specific and parasitic.

Non-specific diseases have no constant cause. A variety of causes may produce the same disease. For example, acute indigestion may be caused by a change of diet, watering the animal after feeding grain, or by exhaustion and intestinal worms. Usually, but one of the animals in the stable or herd is affected. If several are affected, it is because all have been subject to the same condition, and not because the disease has spread from one animal to another.

33   Based on the definition of disease in the first paragraph of the passage we can safely infer that

A   all illnesses are diseases.
B   no injuries are diseases
C   some injuries are diseases.
D   all diseases are illnesses.

34   Non-specific diseases

A   include non-specific viruses.
B   are rarely communicable.
C   are not life-threatening.
D   include accidents.

Passage 2

Questions 35-37

The terms infectious and contagious are used in speaking of specific diseases. Much confusion exists in the popular use of these terms. A contagious disease is one that may be transmitted by personal contact, as, for example, influenza, glanders and hog-cholera. As these diseases may be produced by indirect contact with the diseased animals well as by direct, they are also infectious. There are a few germ diseases that are not spread by the healthy animals coming in direct contact with the diseased animal, as, for example, black leg and southern cattle fever. These are purely infectious diseases. Infection is a more comprehensive term than contagion, as it may be used in alluding to all germ diseases, while the use of the term contagion is rightly limited to such diseases as are produced principally through individual contact.

For convenience we may divide the causes of disease into the predisposing and the exciting.

The predisposing causes are such factors as tend to render the body more susceptible to disease or favour the presence of the exciting cause. For example, an animal that is narrow-chested and lacking in the development of the vital organs lodged in the thoracic cavity, when exposed to the same conditions as the other members of the herd, may contract disease while the animals having better conformation do not. Hogs confined in well-drained yards and pastures that are free from filth, and fed in pens and on feeding floors that are clean, do not become hosts for large numbers of parasites. Hogs confined in filthy pens are frequently so badly infested with lice and intestinal worms that their health and thriftiness are seriously interfered with. Exciting causes usually operate through the environment. With the exception of the special disease-producing germs, the most common exciting causes are faulty food and faulty methods of feeding.

35   The difference between a contagious and an infectious disease is that

A   contagious diseases are transmitted indirectly but infectious diseases can be transmitted directly or indirectly.
B   contagious diseases can be transmitted indirectly or directly, but infectious diseases can only be transmitted indirectly.
C   contagious diseases are not germ diseases, but infectious diseases are contagious diseases.
D   infectious diseases include all contagious diseases, but contagious diseases do not include all infectious diseases.

36   Predisposing causes differ from exciting causes in that

A   predisposing causes are indirect while exciting causes are direct.
B   predisposing causes account for the presence of the disease, while exciting causes exacerbate it.
C   predisposing causes are more difficult to control than exciting causes.
D   exciting causes are more difficult to control than predisposing causes.

37   What increased risks do farmers expose themselves to if, when faced by severe declines in pork prices, they reduce staff to a minimum and switch to lower grade feed?

A   increased risk of contagious diseases such as viruses only.
B   increased risk of infectious diseases such as hoof and mouth only.
C   increased risk of both infectious and contagious diseases.
D   no significant increased risk of infectious or contagious disease

Unit 10

Questions 38-42

The passage below defines middle class socialism and differentiates it from working class or revolutionary socialism.

Passage 1

Questions 38 & 39

Socialism commends itself to a considerable proportion of the working class simply as a beneficial change in the conditions of work and employment; to other sections of the community it presents itself through equally limited aspects. To the stockbroker and many other sorts of trader, to the usurer, to the company promoter, for example, it stands for the dissolution of all comprehensible social order. To great numbers of agreeable and intelligent people who live upon rent and interest it is a projected severing of every bond that holds man and man, that keeps servants respectful, trades-people in order, railways and hotels available, and the whole procedure of life going. They class Socialism and Anarchism together in a way that is as logically unjust as it is from their point of view justifiable. Both cults have this in common, that they threaten to wipe out the whole world of the villa resident.

Some of the most ardent and serviceable of Socialist workers, are philanthropic people, or women and men of the managing temperament shocked into a sort of Socialism by the more glaring and melodramatic cruelties of our universally cruel social system. They are the district visitors of Socialism. They do not realize that Socialism demands any change in themselves or in their way of living, they perceive in it simply a way of hope from the failures of vulgar charity. Chiefly they assail the bad conditions of life of the lower classes. They don't for a moment envisage a time when there will be no lower classes—that is beyond them altogether. Much less can they conceive of a time when there will be no governing class distinctively in possession of means. They exact respect from inferiors; no touch of Socialist warmth or light qualifies their arrogant manners. Perhaps they, too, broaden their conception of Socialism as time goes on, but so it begins with them.

38   Select the statement below that explains why the propertied middle class tends to view Socialism and Anarchism as one and the same.

A   Both doctrines are unprincipled.
B   Both doctrines are anti-capitalist.
C   Both doctrines benefit the poor.
D   Both doctrines are anti-labour.

39   Which phrase below best sums up the author's impression of district socialists as described in the second paragraph of the passage?

A   They are harmless and useless.
B   They are bourgeois and myopic.
C   They are hypocritical and elitists.
D   They are misguided and misinformed.

Passage 2

Questions 40 - 42

Now to make Socialists of this type requires an appeal very different from the talk of class war and expropriation and the abolition of the idle rich, which is so serviceable with a roomful of sweated workers. These people are moved partly by pity, and the best of them by a hatred for the squalor and waste of the present regime. Talk of the expropriated rich simply raises in their minds painful and disconcerting images of distressed gentlewomen. But one necessary aspect of this Socialist's vision that sends the coldest shiver down the spine of the working class Socialist spine is extraordinarily alluring and congenial to them, namely, the official and organized side. They love to think of houses and factories open to competent inspection, of municipal milk, sealed and certificated for every cottager's baby, of old age pensions and a high and rising minimum standard of life. They have an admirable sense of sanitation. They are the philanthropic, administrative Socialists as distinguished from the economic revolutionaries.

This class of Socialist passes insensibly into the merely Socialistic philanthropist of the wealthy middle class to whom we owe so much helpful expenditure upon experiments in housing, in museum, and school construction, in educational endowment, and so forth. They are a constant demonstration to dull and sceptical persons that things may be different, better, prettier, kindlier and more orderly. Many people impervious to tracts can be set thinking by a model village or a model factory. However petty much of what they achieve may be, there it is achieved—in legislation, in bricks and mortar.

Among other things, these administrative Socialists serve to correct the very perceptible tendency of most working men Socialists to sentimental anarchism in regard to questions of control and conduct, a tendency due entirely to their social and administrative inexperience and their commitment to change.

40 Administrative socialists can be said to further the aims of socialism by

A providing the expertise and funding for model villages.
B balancing the needs of the 'haves' and the 'have-nots'.
C actively promoting Socialism in their circles.
D actively promoting Socialism amongst the working class.

41 The author uses the image of the distressed gentlewoman to

A discredit the aims of revolutionary socialists.
B justify the aims of revolutionary socialism.
C critique the commitment of middle class socialists.
D emphasize the human costs of revolutionary socialism.

42 The passage suggests that as opposed to administrative Socialists, working class socialists are

A unruly and disorganized.
B inexperienced and overzealous.
C highly organized, but poorly disciplined.
D ineffectual and inarticulate.

Unit 11

Questions 43 -46

Volunteers, asserts one social services agency specializing in foster care, can have a huge positive impact on the outcomes for children in foster care. Every effort should be made, according to CASA Board President Ernistene Grey to link people who feel they have something to offer children with the children who need them. Not everyone agrees. Read the passage below and the comments from readers that follow to answer the questions.

The findings from a National Online Harris Poll commissioned by the National Court Appointed Special Advocate (CASA) Association show that 87 percent of Americans believe improving foster care should be a national priority. The poll also found that although the community deems the issue important, 83 percent of adults polled know little or nothing about the experiences of children in foster care. Despite their lack of awareness of foster care, 73 percent of adults surveyed agree that they have the potential to positively influence the lives of foster children.

"These are people we — and our foster youth — so desperately need," said National CASA CEO Michael Piraino. "We know that when a CASA volunteer is involved, children are 95 percent less likely to re-enter the foster care system. There are people out there who are willing to help, they just don't know how."

When asked what foster children need, they say it's simple — "We just need someone to be there to listen. We trust people who are willing to listen to us."

"African-American children represent 32 percent of America's 510,000 children in foster care but only 15 percent of the general population. Not only are these children disproportionately overrepresented in foster care, but once in the foster care system, children of colour tend to receive fewer services, stay in care longer and generally have worse outcomes than white children," said Ernestine S. Gray, National CASA Board president and Orleans Parish Juvenile Court Judge in New Orleans.

Comments from readers

Comment I

Congratulations CASA volunteers! 95% of children kept from re-entering foster care! With results like that, we should take whatever it is you do, mass distribute it, and get 95% of children everywhere out of foster care. I cannot help but wonder, though, why our African American children still have such poor foster care outcomes. Could it be like the rest of the foster care conglomerate, CASA ignores them too, or is CASA merely exaggerating?

(signed) Confused

Comment II

I thought I was ready to be a foster parent, and went through all kinds of hoops to qualify—police checks, home inspections, training and education. In the end though, I was no way prepared for the foster kids I got! They were monsters, and one after the other I had to ship them back. To those of you thinking to work with foster kids I have one word: BEWARE!

(signed) Worn out in Walawala

Comment III

I can just imagine the paedophiles flooding the phone lines in their rush to volunteer! 'Vulnerable children who trust anyone who will merely listen to them.' Really??? This reads like an invitation to trouble not a solution to our foster care crisis, and CASA should know better. The risks of volunteerism often outweigh the benefits, and this is the very reason that not every Tom, Dick and Harry who feels he has something to offer foster kids can be trusted. We need more care in the system, but ultimately the best care comes from families with a vested interest in their children, not from strangers with an interest in God-knows-what. If you want to help foster children, protect them first and foremost.

(signed) Been There

Comment IV

The first order of business, I should think, would be to make people knowledgeable of foster care, then ask them their opinions. What does a poll in which 83% of the people admit they do not know what they are talking about really tell us? How can we know if we have something to offer foster kids if we don't know the first thing about their needs? It is this kind of data that gets us all in trouble.

(signed) Keep it Real

43   We may safely infer from the data given that of those polled about foster care,

A   73% of those polled are willing to help improve foster care.
B   13% of those polled feel foster care is adequate as is.
C   4% of respondents fully understood the poll.
D   68% of children in foster care are not African American.

44   The principle aim of the passage is to.

A   expose deficiencies in the foster care system.
B   expose inequalities in the foster care system.
C   lobby for government funding for foster care.
D   lobby for CASA foster care volunteers.

45 Which of the comments that follow the article addresses the claims of the article and which address the aims of the article?

A   Comments I and IV address article's aims, while comments III and IV address its claims.
B   Comments II and III address the article's aims, while comments I and IV address its claims.
C   Comments I and IV address the articles claims, while comments II and III address its aims.
D   Comments II and IV address the article's aims, while articles I and III address its claims.

46 Which of the four comments does not expose a risk associated with foster care volunteerism?

A   Comment I
B   Comment II
C   Comment III
D   Comment IV

Unit 12

Questions 47-50

The passage below explains tribal connections amongst ancient European groups and delineates the ties that possibly bind them.

Questions 47-50

We learn from a passage in the *Germania* of Tacitus' that certain tribes of Heilgoland agreed with each other in the worship of a goddess who was revered as 'Earth the Mother'; that a sacred grove, in a sacred island, was dedicated to her; and that, in that grove, there stood a holy wagon, covered with a pall, and touched by the priest only. The goddess herself was drawn by heifers; and as long as she vouchsafed her presence among men, there was joy, and feasts, and hospitality; and peace amongst otherwise fierce tribes instead of war and violence. After a time, however, the goddess withdrew herself to her secret temple--satiated with the converse of mankind; and then the wagon, the pall, and the deity herself were bathed in the holy lake. The administrant slaves were sucked up by its waters. There was terror and there was ignorance; the reality being revealed to those alone who thus suddenly passed from life to death.

Now we know, by name at least, five of the tribes who are thus connected by a common worship--mysterious and obscure as it is. They are the Reudigni, the Aviones, the Eudoses, the Suardones, and the Nuithones. Two others we know by something more than name--the Varini and the Langobardi. The eighth is our own parent stock--the Angli.

Like ancient Venetians, the Angli are characterized by an utter absence of horses, mules, ponies, asses, carts, wagons, or any of the ordinary applications of animal power to the purposes of locomotion, confined to a small rock, and but little interrupted with foreign elements. But what if the source of its population be other than that which, from the occupants of the nearest portion of the continent, we are prepared to expect?

When the populations differ, one of two views has to be taken. On one hand we can say that a change has taken in the expected pattern of migration, on the other, that a change has taken place on the part of one or both of the populations since the period of the original migration.

47   We can safely infer that the worship of the Earth the Mother goddess

A   maintained discipline and social order amongst the tribes.
B   was accompanied by slavery and human sacrificial rituals.
C   results from a shared ancestry amongst the 8 tribes who worshipped her.
D   evinces a shared ethnology amongst the 8 tribes who worshipped her.

48   The Angli population, *per se*,

A   is relatively insignificant to the ethnographer.
B   is of vast interest to the ethnographer.
C   derives from the ancient Venetians.
D   was heavily influenced the ancient Venetians.

49   As regards to the population of islands, based on the passage, we would tend to expect inhabitants to derive from the

A   nearest mainland.
B   nearest large island.
C   a single gene pool.
D   diverse backgrounds.

50   Which of the following statements, if not true, would have no impact on the authors' premise that the eight tribes mentioned are connected ethnographically by their worship of the Earth Mother goddess?

A   The 8 ancient tribes worshipped an Earth Mother goddess.
B   Ancient Venetians have much in common with the Angli.
C   The Angli were not influenced by diverse foreign elements.
D   The Angli were a generally isolated people.

Unit 13

Questions 51 & 52

Inflationary pressure

51 If the data represents the economy, the cartoon suggests that

A peak tolerable levels of inflation have been reached.
B peak tolerable levels of inflation are about to be reached.
C inflation is caused by overconsumption.
D inflation is caused by the white middle class.

52 Which of the following is not a factor developed in the cartoon?

A the cause of inflation
B the effect of inflation
C the solution to inflation
D the ironies of inflation

Unit 14

Questions 53-55

Healthcare providers, particularly those in developing countries with limited resources, are faced with a true dilemma when deciding how to prioritize healthcare spending. Read the passage below that discusses the need to prioritize primary health care without detracting from secondary and tertiary care in developing countries and answer the questions that follow.

Healthcare professionals around the world are painfully aware that governments and the medical community must work together to support primary healthcare, but not at the cost of curative and specialist services. None-the-less, little progress has been made worldwide as regards improving preventative care. Brain drain is one issue. Despite the protests of developing governments that they are robbed of the best of their health staff, doctors and nurses continue to emigrate in alarming numbers. Most health care professionals are committed to the concept of helping others and naturally want to work within a system that provides better health and better health care responses to the general population. They cannot wait indefinitely and, perhaps, in vain for the health systems in their countries to function properly. Those who stay seek the higher salaried and more prestigious specialist and private sector positions contributing to in-country brain drain and leaving primary care in the lurch. Organizations on the frontline of public health such as the World Health Organization (WHO) also call for a return to primary healthcare approaches as this level of care has proved to adequately address health issues in developed and developing countries. Primary care is the focus of WHO as a means of solving health issues as opposed to curative care which is far more costly and is increasingly overwhelming healthcare systems around the world. A US report on climate change notes that health issues arising from climate change can adequately be addressed at the primary level. This just goes to show what strengthening the primary health care system can do. WHO's claim that preventative services could reduce the occurrence of global disease is no myth, as no other organization is authorized to make this claim.

Tackling public health issues and leading the fight against preventable diseases and epidemics is simply not within the purview of the secondary and tertiary healthcare systems. It is only logical that more resources be allocated to the primary system which is capable of preventing up to 70% of the disease burden. Despite the need to provide secondary and tertiary care, it is high time governments prioritize spending on preventive services so that the majority of people can access care according to their needs and regardless of their ability to pay before they become seriously ill. This is one of the ways out of the health challenges faced by developing countries and the only way out of poverty in the long term.

53 Based on the findings of the US report on climate change stating that primary care systems can manage health problems associated with climate change we can safely infer that

A   most health risks associated with climate change are minimal.
B   most health risks associated with climate change are preventable.
C   the US invests more heavily in primary than in secondary or tertiary care.
D   climate change is likely to more directly impact the US than other countries.

54 On the strength of the evidence provided in the passage we can safely infer that WHO's claim that a global focus on preventative care could reduce the overall occurrence of global disease is

A   valid given the fact that only WHO can make such a claim and has clearly done so.
B   myth, as the claim cannot be proved until the global focus shifts to preventative care.
C   invalid, as the evidence provided in support of the claim is extraneous to the claim.
D   probably valid given the status and stature of WHO as regards global health initiatives.

55 If the author's reasoning is sound,

A   widespread poverty in developing countries causes poor health and preventable epidemics.
B   primary care costs more to provide than secondary or tertiary care in developing countries.
C   secondary and tertiary care cost more to provide than primary care in developing countries.
D   prioritizing secondary and tertiary care in developing countries causes illness and poverty.

Unit 15:

Questions 56-61

The passages below introduce readers to Winston Smith, the protagonist of George Orwell's 1949 classic novel, *1984*. The setting is a futuristic dystopian society named 'Oceanian province of Airstrip One' (formerly known as Great Britain).

Passage 1

Questions 56 & 57

Winston kept his back turned to the telescreen. It was safer; though, as he well knew, even a back can be revealing. A kilometre away the Ministry of Truth, his place of work, towered vast and white above the grimy landscape. This, he thought with a sort of vague distaste--this was London, chief city of Airstrip One, itself the third most populous of the provinces of Oceania.

The Ministry of Truth -Minitrue, in Newspeak- was startlingly different from any other object in sight. It was an enormous pyramidal structure of glittering white concrete, soaring up, terrace after terrace, 300 metres into the air. From where Winston stood it was just possible to read, picked out on its white face in elegant lettering, the three slogans of the Party:

WAR IS PEACE
FREEDOM IS SLAVERY
IGNORANCE IS STRENGTH

Winston turned round abruptly. He had set his features into the expression of quiet optimism which it was advisable to wear when facing the telescreen. He crossed the room into the tiny kitchen. By leaving the Ministry at this time of day he had sacrificed his lunch in the canteen, and he was aware that there was no food in the kitchen except a hunk of dark-coloured bread which had got to be saved for tomorrow's breakfast. He took down from the shelf a bottle of colourless liquid with a plain white label marked VICTORY GIN. It gave off a sickly, oily smell, as of Chinese rice-spirit. Winston poured out nearly a teacupful, nerved himself for a shock, and gulped it down like a dose of medicine.

Instantly his face turned scarlet and the water ran out of his eyes. The stuff was like nitric acid, and moreover, in swallowing it one had the sensation of being hit on the back of the head with a rubber club. The next moment, however, the burning in his belly died down and the world began to look more cheerful.

He went back to the living-room and sat down at a small table that stood to the left of the telescreen. From the table drawer he took out a penholder, a bottle of ink, and a thick, quarto-sized blank book with a red back and a marbled cover.

56 Consider the four types of central conflicts present in literature below to determine the level of conflict prevalent in the passage.

A   protagonist versus self
B   protagonist versus another
C   protagonist versus environment
D   protagonist versus God, fate or universal forces

57 Winston Smith can best be described as being

A   defiant
B   deliberate
C   depressed
D   dehumanized

Passage 2

Questions 58-61

For some reason the telescreen in the living-room was in an unusual position. Instead of being placed, as was normal, in the end wall, where it could command the whole room, it was in the longer wall, opposite the window. To one side of it there was a shallow alcove in which Winston was now sitting, and which, when the flats were built, had probably been intended to hold bookshelves. It was partly the unusual geography of the room that had suggested to him the thing that he was now about to do.

But it had also been suggested by the book that he had just taken out of the drawer. It was a peculiarly beautiful book. Its smooth creamy paper, a little yellowed by age, was of a kind that had not been manufactured for at least forty years past. He could guess, however, that the book was much older than that. He had seen it lying in the window of a frowsy little junk-shop in a slummy quarter of the town (just what quarter he did not now remember) and had been stricken immediately by an overwhelming desire to possess it. Party members were supposed not to go into ordinary shops ('dealing on the free market', it was called), but the rule was not strictly kept, because there were various things, such as shoelaces and razor blades, which it was impossible to get hold of in any other way. He had given a quick glance up and down the street and then had slipped inside and bought the book for two dollars fifty.

The thing that he was about to do was to open a diary. This was not illegal (nothing was illegal, since there were no longer any laws), but if detected it was reasonably certain that it would be punished by death, or at least by twenty-five years in a forced-labour camp. Winston fitted a nib into the penholder and sucked it to get the grease off. Actually he was not used to writing by hand. Apart from very short notes, it was usual to dictate everything into the speak-write which was of course impossible for his present purpose. He dipped the pen into the ink and then faltered for just a second. A tremor had gone through his bowels. To mark the paper was the decisive act. In small clumsy letters he wrote:

April 4th, 1984.

58   Consider the four personality types and motives presented in the table below and answer the question that follows:

Personality Type: Intrinsic/personal **Motivated by:** Personal satisfaction	**Personality Type:** Intrinsic interpersonal **Motivated by:** Social Interaction
Personality Type: Extrinsic/personal **Motivated by:** Personal Rewards	**Personality Type:** Extrinsic/interpersonal **Motivated by:** Public Recognition.

Which of the four personality types in the table above is Winston Smith?

- A   intrinsic/personal
- B   intrinsic/interpersonal
- C   extrinsic/personal
- D   extrinsic/interpersonal

59   If the climax of a work is that point when the central conflict of the passage is resolved, we can say that this passage reaches its climax when Winston

- A   comes home for lunch.
- B   hides in the alcove.
- C   opens the book.
- D   writes the date.

60   We can safely infer that when he sits in the alcove, Winston Smith can

- A   see the telescreen but not be seen by it.
- B   be seen but not heard in the alcove.
- C   not be seen or heard in the alcove.
- D   not see the telescreen or be seen by it.

61 If coincidence can be fairly used to further the action of a story but cannot fairly be used to resolve the central conflict, we can say that the placement of the telescreen

A constitutes fair use of coincidence in the passage.
B is not coincidental as its placement is logically explained.
C is not coincidental because all flats have a blind spot.
D constitutes unfair use of coincidence in the passage.

Unit 16

Questions 62-64

A majority of those surveyed say they are willing to pay 34% more for their clothing to help eradicate child labour. However, putting an end to child labour is not, at least according to one international organization, that easy. Read the passage below and answer the questions that follow.

According to a survey released by Child Fund International about child labour, of 1,022 people surveyed, the average consumer guesses that only 6.5 million children aged 5 to 14 are child labourers and 73 percent of survey respondents say there are fewer than 1 million. Only 1 percent accurately estimate the correct number of child labourers - 150 million. Of these 150 million, 25.6% are engaged in service, 7% in industry/manufacturing, 7.5% in mining and 60% in agriculture.

With knowledge comes power - spending power. When asked if they would be willing to pay more for clothing made without child labour, more than half (55 percent) indicate that they would—up to one third (34%) more.

"This spring's collapse of a garment factory in Bangladesh has focused the world's attention on the often hazardous working conditions that many workers in developing countries confront every day, and while it appears that the more than 1,000 victims of that tragedy were adults, the fact is these factories regularly employ children as young as 10 years old," says Anne Lynam Goddard, president and CEO of Child Fund International.

Almost one in six children ages 5 to 14 in developing countries is engaged in labour, and aside from the obvious physical dangers that young children face in hazardous working conditions, these children are less likely to complete their educations. The hours they spend working are hours they cannot devote to their studies.

Child labour has always existed, and on some level it always will, Goddard explains, emphasizing that not all labour is exploitative or necessarily harmful to children and noting that many children within developing countries must work on their families' subsistence farms or engage in other labour to supplement family income. Child labour was widely practiced in developed countries until these countries adopted compulsory, universal education laws.

Furthermore, if the child's earnings are keeping a family alive, then it is unethical to fire that child. Well known 'green' and designer brands wishing to distance themselves from the taint of child labour employ children but provide them with food and free education. 'This is safe and ethical and better than the logical alternatives, death or prostitution' explains Goddard. 'Our concern,' she says, 'is when a child is compelled to work in unsafe conditions or when work serves to interrupt his or her education'.

62 It can be safely inferred from the data provided by the Child Fund survey that

A   child labour can be abolished globally without harming labourers, consumers, or producers.
B   child labour will never be abolished but can be regulated to eventually become an ethical form of labour.
C   industrialist owners reap the benefits of child labour while keeping consumers in the dark.
D   the majority react emotionally to the issue, rejecting child labour without understanding it.

63 Consumers' willingness to pay up to one third more for clothing, if implemented would

A   put an end to the most dangerous forms of child labour.
B   have minimal impact on the numbers or safety of child labourers.
C   abate poverty by ensuring that more children enrol and stay in school.
D   result in lower mortality rates amongst the world's child labourers.

64 Consider each of the statements below in light of the passage above and answer the question that follows.

I   Consumers fuel the need for child labour.
II   Child labour can be eradicated by educating the public.
III Child Fund supports some forms of child labour.
IV   Families that send their children to work are the root cause of child labour.
V   Compulsory education for all children is the cure to child labour.

Which of the statements above is supported by the passage?

A   Statements I and III
B   Statements II and IV
C   Statements III and V
D   Statements II and V

Unit 17

Questions 65 & 66

Consider the cartoon and the definitions of irony provided in the table that follows to answer the questions below.

Open day at the abbottoir

Situational Irony	Dramatic Irony	Verbal Irony
An event of outcome of events opposite to what was or might naturally have been expected.	One of the characters is unaware of or oblivious to important information that the audience is aware of.	What is said is different from and usually opposite of what is meant.

65 As regards the irony used in the cartoon, we can safely say that

A all 3 kinds of irony from the table are utilized in the cartoon.
B only situational irony is utilized in the cartoon.
C only situational and dramatic irony are utilized in the cartoon.
D only situational and verbal irony are utilized in the cartoon.

66 As used in the cartoon, the word abattoir is

A synonymous with monastery.
B synonymous with slaughterhouse.
C used sarcastically.
D used ironically.

Unit 18:

Questions 67-72

Passage 1

Questions 67 & 68

Modern English, according to the author of the passage below, has become slovenly just as modern culture and politics have. Read the passage below and answer the questions that follow.

Most people who bother with the matter at all would admit that the English language is in a bad way, but it is generally assumed that we cannot by conscious action do anything about it. Our civilization is decadent, and our language--so the argument runs--must inevitably share in the general collapse. It follows that any struggle against the abuse of language is a sentimental archaism, like preferring candles to electric light or hansom cabs to aeroplanes.

Now, it is clear that the decline of a language must ultimately have political and economic causes: it is not due simply to the bad influence of this or that individual writer. But an effect can become a cause-reinforcing the original cause and producing the same effect in an intensified form, and so on indefinitely. A man may take to drink because he feels himself to be a failure, and then fail all the more completely because he drinks. It is rather the same thing that is happening to the English language. It becomes ugly and inaccurate because our thoughts are foolish, but the slovenliness of our language makes it easier for us to have foolish thoughts. The point is that the process is reversible.

Modern English, especially written English, is full of bad habits which spread by imitation and which can be avoided if one is willing to take the necessary trouble. If one gets rid of these habits one can think more clearly, and to think clearly is a necessary first step towards political regeneration: so that the fight against bad English is not frivolous and is not the exclusive concern of professional writers. I will come back to this presently, and I hope that by that time the meaning of what I have said here will have become clearer.

67   Underlying most people's beliefs about the English language is the assumption that language is

A   a natural growth and not an instrument.
B   an instrument, not a natural growth
C   the master of man rather than the reverse.
D   the result of a general decline in the level of writing.

68   The causal relationship described in the second paragraph can best be described as

A   a parody.
B   a paradox.
C   a self-fulfilling prophecy.
D   a self-serving prophecy.

Passage 2

Questions 69-72

Meanwhile, here are five specimens of the English language as it is now habitually written.

These four passages have not been picked out because they are especially bad--I could have quoted far worse if I had chosen--but because they illustrate several of the mental vices from which we now suffer.

Example 1

> I am not, indeed, sure whether it is not true to say that the Milton who once seemed not unlike a seventeenth-century Shelley had not become, out of an experience ever more bitter in each year, more alien to the founder of that Jesuit sect which nothing could induce him to tolerate.
>
> *PROFESSOR HAROLD LASKI (Essay in Freedom of Expression)*

Example 2

> Above all, we cannot play ducks and drakes with a native battery of idioms which prescribes such egregious collocations of vocables as the Basic put up with or tolerate or put at a loss or bewilder.

PROFESSOR LANCELOT HOGBEN (Interglossa)

Example 3

On the one side we have the free personality; by definition it is not neurotic, for it has neither conflict nor dream. Its desires, such as they are, are transparent, for they are just what institutional approval keeps in the forefront of consciousness; another institutional pattern would alter their number and intensity; there is little in them that is natural, irreducible, or culturally dangerous. But on the other side, the social bond itself is nothing but the mutual reflection of these self-secure integrities. Recall the definition of love. Is not this the very picture of a small academic? Where is there a place in this hall of mirrors for either personality or fraternity?

ESSAY ON PSYCHOLOGY in Politics (New York)

Example 4

All the 'best people' from the gentlemen's clubs, and all the frantic fascist captains, united in common hatred of Socialism and bestial horror of the rising tide of the mass revolutionary movement, have turned to acts of provocation, to foul incendiarism, to medieval legends of poisoned wells, to legalize their own destruction of proletarian organizations, and rouse the agitated petty-bourgeoisie to chauvinistic fervour on behalf of the fight against the revolutionary way out of the crisis.
COMMUNIST PAMPHLET

69 Which of the following can we safely infer from Example 1?

A   Milton could not tolerate Shelly.
B   Milton could not tolerate the founder of the Jesuit sect.
C   Milton could not tolerate the Jesuit sect.
D   Milton could not tolerate his bitter life.

70 Which of the four comments actually exemplifies the very problem it criticizes?

A   Example 1
B   Example 2
C   Example 3
D   Example 4

71 If the modern man's mental vices are present in the examples provided by the author, we can say that our vices include all but

A   hyperbolic raving.
B   obtuse references.
C   prudent conservation.
D   garrulous circumlocution.

72 The fight mentioned at the end of example 4 refers to the fight

A   against the petty-bourgeoisie.
B   for communism.
C   for the socialist revolution.
D   against socialism.

Unit 19

Questions 73 - 75

The passage below explores correlations between nutrition and physical degeneration amongst native Australians living in government reservations and relegated to a government prescribed diet.

An interesting incident was brought to my attention in one of the Australian reservations where the food was provided entirely by the government. I was told by the director in charge, and in further detail by the other officials, that a number of native babies had become ill while nursing from their mothers. Some had died. By changing the nutrition to a condensed whole milk product, the babies recovered. When placed back on their mother's breast, they again became ill. The problem was: Why was not their mothers' milk adequate? I was later told by the director of a condition that had developed in the pen of the reservation's hogs which were kept to use up the scraps and garbage from the reservation's kitchens. He reported that one after another the hogs went down with a type of paralysis and could not get up. The symptoms were suggestively like vitamin A deficiency in both the babies and the hogs, and indicated the treatment.

The rapid degeneration of the Australian Aborigines after the adoption of the government's modern foods provides a demonstration that should be infinitely more convincing than animal experimentation. It should be a matter not only of concern but deep alarm that human beings can degenerate physically so rapidly by the use of a certain type of nutrition, particularly the dietary products used so generally by modern civilization.

Another important source of information regarding the Aborigines of Australia was provided by a study of the skeletal material and skulls in the museums at Sydney and Canberra, particularly the former. I do not know the number of skulls that are available there for study, but it is very large, making one wonder about the true motives behind it. I examined many and found them remarkably uniform in design and quality. The dental arches were splendidly formed. The teeth were in excellent condition with exceedingly little dental caries. A characteristic of these skulls was the evidence of a shortage of material for those that had been transferred to a museum from the interior arid plains country. Those skulls, however, that had come from coastal areas where sea foods were available, show much more massive dimensions of the general pattern.

73 Which of the following statements, if true, supports the narrator's premise that the hogs and women on the Australian reservation he visited both suffered from vitamin A deficiency caused by a deficient diet?

A   The hogs ate table scraps and grain.
B   The hogs ate table scraps only.
C   The hog's diet was adequate.
D   The hogs were allowed to forage for food.

74 Native Australians' rapid physical degeneration after switching to the government food supply strongly suggests that

A   the government sought to reduce numbers of native Australians by intentionally putting them on a deficient diet.
B   the food supplied was nutritionally inadequate to meet human nutritional needs.
C   nutritional needs of native and non-native Australians vary substantially.
D   native Australians found the food distasteful, refused to eat it and inadvertently caused their own nutritional problems.

75 The author's mention of the very large collection of skeletal material and skulls

A   suggests the heads were severed.
B   is a subtle critique of colonization.
C   demonstrates the comprehensive nature of his study.
D   is a barely cloaked racial slur.

Solutions to Practice Questions ANSWERS

Unit 1

1   Option A can be eliminated as discursive (empiric or scientific) knowledge relies on the senses (what we see, feel, can touch, measure, manipulate etc.) while coercive knowledge derived from mystic intuition relies on an inner passion that is extra-sensory. In light of this statement, it is clear that option B is supported by the passage: discursive knowledge relies on the senses, while coercive knowledge is extra-sensory. Like option A, option C must be eliminated. There is no way of knowing for sure which route to knowledge is quickest, but the passage makes clear that coercive, not discursive, insights are sudden. Furthermore, there is no suggestion that coercive insights negate what we have learned from discursive, scientific processes. Discursive knowledge is not based on insight, as stated in option D, but on observation, meaning that this option must also be eliminated.
Correct Answer: B

2   Intuitive illumination provides a more sublime vision of reality, but it is not the only way to understand reality as stated in option A. Neither does the passage support the statement that only mystics truly understand reality (option B). The visionary world of the mystic is 'utterly different' from reality as we know it, not a reflection of it as stated in C. The author refers to the illusionary reality of the mystic as being far superior to discursive reality which includes all to the 'follies and wickedness of man'. Discursive reality is the moment of glory and the haunting beauty and the faint reflection of the sun. Clearly the author feels it is the preferable state.
Correct Answer D

3   It is the impulse towards unity or the 'denial of a universal division or opposition' (option A) that fuels the mystic's tendency to deny the existence of time. If all is the same, there is no past, present or future, and all time is one. The passage does not speak explicitly to the disparity of human experience (B), but if there is universal unity, we can assume that there is no disparity of human experience whatsoever. The plurality of good and evil is consistent with the mystic vision of unity, but has nothing at all to do with the mystic apprehension time. Hence, D must be eliminated.
Correct answer: A

4   The author tells us that 'mysticism is to be commended as an attitude towards life, not as a creed about the world', and he calls it a 'mistaken outcome of the emotion'. From this we can safely infer he is a rationalist with mystic impulses rather than a mystic with empirical impulses as stated in A. He does not reject mystic impulses (B), saying instead that mystic apprehension likely inspires whatever is best in mankind. Mysticism, the author tells us, is a mistaken outcome of emotion, but he does not tell us that it is a mistaken response to reality (C). As the author believes that 'mysticism is to be commended as an attitude towards life, not as a creed about the world'. He is, then, a rationalist who is sympathetic to (mystic) intuition (D).
Correct Answer: D

Unit 2

5   The government seems to have impeded the approval and distribution of genetically modified fish with unnecessary 'political gridlock' over the last 18 years. Option A, then, can be eliminated. The government is vigilant, perhaps overly so, but option B, that the government is determined to keep genetically modified animals off the market is clearly an overstatement. The author clearly views government scrutiny as red-tape and gridlock, and he clearly agrees with expert assessments that genetically modified fish is safe and beneficial, supporting option C. Option D must be eliminated as it is not adequately supported by the passage. The author clearly reports that government has been overly vigilant, causing gridlock and unnecessary delays in the approval process, but this complaint is documented in the passage and not necessarily the result of authorial bias.
Correct Answer: C

6   Dr Mark Walton began the non-profit Feed the Real World, but this does not tell us much about his real motives or goals in developing a 'better' (genetically modified) salmon. Option A is not adequately supported. Option B must also be eliminated. Dr Walton is clearly frustrated by governmental bureaucratic delays, but the passage does not tell us if he welcomes or eschews the scrutiny of the scientific community. He believes the process has been subverted by commercial and political interests, suggesting that government is <u>not</u> acting in the best interests of consumers who would benefit from more plentiful and potentially cheaper salmon. C, then, is supported by the passage. Despite his frustration with the regulatory process, there is no suggestion that Dr Walton feels government has no viable role in the regulation of the biotechnology industry (D).
Correct Answer: C

7   Although the American public is clearly generally wary of genetically modified foods, this does not seem to be a concern shared by the scientific community that has come out in support of the modified salmon. A, then, must be eliminated. There is no indication that government lacks the special technology required to calculate the risks associated with farming genetically modified salmon (B). That genetically modified fish pose 'minimal environmental risk' (C) implies that they pose some environmental risk. Albeit unlikely, there is still some chance that genetically modified salmon escape and have an impact on the environment. C, then, is supported. Option D is alluded to with the reference to commercial interests acting to delay the approval process, but the passage does not explicitly state that the modified salmon will undermine the fishing industry and D must be eliminated.
Correct Answer: C

Unit 3

8   Option A must be eliminated. Whereas 90% of all slaves shipped to Brazil derived from Gambia, only 50 passages were made from this port, and there is no way of determining the total number of slaves sent to Brazil. It is quite likely that the number of slaves shipped to other destinations from Sierra Leon (with 107 passages) or Bight of Biafra (with 111 passages) far out number of slaves sent from Gambia to Brazil. Option B, however, is supported by the passage. If Cuba received no more than 10% of its slaves from any given port of embarkation, each

representing a different catchment area with a unique demographic, it is reasonable to infer that slaves reaching Cuba came from all over Africa and represented the most ethnic diversity. C must be eliminated as the passage does not speak to steps shipmasters could take to reduce mortality rates during passage. The passage makes clear that best shipmasters could do was to try to secure work from destinations with historically lower mortality rates. Option D must be eliminated. 13% of all slaves overall died in port or in transport, but this is an average and does not mean that each passage had 13% mortality rates.
Correct Answer: B

9   To answer this question correctly, candidates must look for the single factor among those given that is consistently associated with higher mortality rates. The duration of the passage (option A) would indeed seem to be an important factor, but according to the data, duration is not a consistent deciding factor. Congo/Angola, for example, with an average of 66 days spent in passage has nearly double the mortality rates of Sierra Leone with a 75 day passage. Option A, then, can be eliminated. The percentage of males on board, or male to female ratio (option B), on the other hand, can be linked to higher slave mortality in port and during passage. The two ports of embarkation with the highest percentage of female slaves, Congo/Angola and Bight of Biafra, also have the highest mortality rates. The number of overall passages (option C) does not seem to consistently affect mortality rates. Sierra Leone with 107 passages has higher overall mortality rates than ports with fewer passages such as Gambia and the Gold Coast, and Senegambia, with the fewest passages, does not have the lowest mortality rates. Similarly we can draw no parallels between the number of days spent in port (option D) and higher mortality. The Gold Coast, with an average of 99 days spent in port has the second lowest overall mortality rates, while Sierra Leone with only 58 days in port has only the third lowest mortality rate.
Correct answer: B

10   Basic math reveals that Statement I is true. A total of 33.0% of slaves died in port while a total of 27.7% of all slaves died in passage. Statement II is also true. The point of the data is that passages from some ports were statistically more successful in terms of mortality than passages from other ports. Statement III, however, is not supported by the data. As we do not know total numbers of slaves transported, we have no way of knowing which ports provided the highest number of female slaves. Like statement III, statement IV is not supported. Indeed, Bight of Biafra saw the highest number of passages overall, but as we do not know the numbers of slaves on any passage, we have no way of knowing the total numbers of slaves shipped from any port. Statement IV is supported by the data. We see that the two ports with the lowest percentage of males on board also have the highest mortality rates, suggesting a correlation between a higher percentage of women and higher mortality rates. As statements I, II and V are supported by the data, option C is the correct answer.
Correct Answer: C

Unit 4

11   Whereas the author tells us that humans must adapt to other humans to succeed in the modern environment, he does not go so far as to say that we are becoming more socially adaptable as a species in the process. The author tells us, further, that man has been more

successful than any other creature at adapting to his environment in the past, but this does not tell us if he will continue to be so successful in adapting to his new environmental challenge: his fellow man. Option A, then, is not supported by the passage. According to the author we develop the body type our personality requires; for each group of (personality) traits there are external, physical indicators. Hence personality dictates body type and option B is supported. He goes on, with the description of the terrier and the St. Bernard to illustrate that physical makeup, or body type, invariably indicates the internal, or personality type. Option C is also supported. As the environment dictates physical characteristics and our personality, we can infer, following the author's line of thinking, that people from a given village would face the same environmental challenges and consequently share physical and personal characteristics. They will develop similar physical characteristics and act similarly. Option D, like B and C, is supported.
Correct Answer: A

12 The author alludes to the difference between races in terms of their physical and emotional makeup, brought about by their specific environment, but he does not give preference to any given race. We cannot, therefore, describe him or his views as being ethnocentric (A). The author clearly considers man the most successful of all creatures, and his elevated view of humans can be described as being anthropocentric (B). The author speaks to differences between peoples from different environments, but he does so without the fear characteristic of the xenophobic (C). Finally, we cannot say the author's views are anthropoidal as this would mean that they belong to a group of various primates who stand erect or semi-erect.
Correct Answer: B

13 The author maintains that it is easy to judge people based on their physical characteristics, or that you can judge a book by its cover. Option A is not supported. He maintains that we develop specific characteristics as a result of our personalities, but that once we have these characteristics, they tend to express themselves—whether we like it or not. Thus, it would be difficult, if not impossible to change, and option B must be eliminated. Appearances, the author tells us, are highly accurate in predicting behaviours and not deceiving as stated in C. Seeing someone is enough for those who know how to 'read' the signs to know what they are like and how they will behave. Option D, then, is consistent with the author's views.
Correct Answer: D

14 According to the passage, man's large jaw is the result of his ancestral need to defend himself, a need that has declined as man has become more civilized. It is not the result of fighting (A) per se. A large jaw today, the author tells us, indicates the owner is prone to fight. He is, then, likely to be anti-social (B) and pugilistic (C). Large jaws are, as stated, the result of ancestry (D). As only option A is not supported, it is the correct answer.
Correct Answer: A

15 Logic fallacies abound in this article, but it is the candidate's task to determine which of the fallacies presented in the table is NOT present in the argument. The author argues his case fallaciously but does not base his premise on the ad populum fallacy (A); he does not try to convince readers of his theory by suggesting that most people already believe that physical appearance is an accurate predictor of personality and behaviour and visa versa but seeks to make his 'science' better known so that more people can believe it. The author does, however,

create a false analogy (B) when he uses differences in dog breeds to explain differences in human races. The author also engages in cherry picking (C) in elaborating his argument. He completely overlooks facts such as the fact that many people with small jaws are highly pugilistic and many people with large jaws are pacifists. The author also engages in the association fallacy (D) in his assumption that people and dogs can be compared, and generalizing from that assumption that all large-jawed people are inherently fighters. As ad populum is the only fallacy not employed, A is the correct answer.
Correct Answer: A

Unit 5

16   Although clearly 'uncivilized', Little Flower seems quite content, and there is no indication that she needs to be discovered or assisted by Pretre. The author is not telling us that she condones colonization when it benefits local populations (A). Neither, however, does she condemn Pretre for his colonialist perspectives (B). The author, rather, reports very objectively, making it clear that she aims to chronicle rather than comment on the encounter (C). As the author reports objectively without expressing sympathy for either the colonizer or the colonized, option D can be eliminated.
Correct Answer: C

17   Pretre is, indeed, impressed by Little Flower's size but it is not really her size (D) that inspires his fascination with her. Neither does his commitment to his profession (A) explain his fascination. After all, we don't know how committed to he is to his profession. Little Flower is exquisitely small, but there is no suggestion she is beautiful (C). In fact, she 'looks like a dog' and 'gives one woman the creeps'. We see from their first encounter that Pretre immediately thinks of Little Flower as an extremely rare and highly valuable discovery. He objectifies her (B) and considers her an object he can own, like a rare gem.
Correct Answer: B

18   Looking carefully at the interactions of Pretre and Little Flower we see that the relationship is one sided. He is definitely more impressed with her than she is with him. He also objectifies her, thinking of her as his possession. This is not, then, a symbiotic relationship as stated in A. Little Flower seems unimpressed in extreme with Pretre when she scratches herself, suggesting that this is not a case of mutual infatuation (C) either. There is no indication that she intends to exploit him (B). Pretre virtually swoons in the presence of Little Flower and is overcome with tenderness for her. As this is emotion is unprovoked and entirely unrequited, it is clear that the relationship is all in Pretre's head (D).
Correct Answer: D

19   Pretre is studying the belly of the smallest woman in the world when he starts to feel sick, but it is not her belly or the fear that she will die in labour (B) that prompts this reaction. The author does not suggest that Pretre suddenly realizes he loves this tiny, gravid woman (C) or that she loves him (D). Little Flower's laughter is what nauseates Pretre. He realizes, as he hears her laugh, that she is human and that she loves, or at very least, enjoys her life. For her, it is enough simply not to be devoured, and Pretre plans, in a metaphorical sense, to devour her by exploiting

her. Her laughter, however, reminds him that she is a human being who loves her life (A), and this new awareness causes him to feel nauseous.
Correct Answer: A

20   Little Flower seems unconcerned, even unaware of her impending delivery (A) so this is not what makes her laugh. She laughs simply because she isn't being devoured; she is, in short, enjoying her unembellished existence (B) at that very moment, and not because she dreams of a better life. Little Flower is moved by love, and this too causes her to laugh, but option D must be eliminated as it is love in general (profound love for the explorer, his boots, his ring...) not love specifically for Pretre that causes her to feel happy.
Correct Answer: B

21   Little Flower loves the explorer profoundly; the author tells us this directly. Being innocent, she is incapable of anything but a profound, unquestioning love that is unconditional (A) and equally applied to all she sees. If A is correct, option B must be eliminated. Despite the unique character of her relationship with Pretre—nothing in the passage suggests that the love Little Flower feels is perverse(C). Neither is her love unrequited (D). We have seen already that Pretre has strong feelings for Little Flower, and nothing in this passage suggests those feelings have changed.
Correct Answer: A

Unit 6

22   The US does not use embryonic stem cells and neither do other countries, suggesting that their policies pertaining to embryonic cells are the same (A), not different (B). We do not know the specific forces behind the US block on embryonic stem cell research from the passage, nor does the graph support the idea that conservative religious groups overwhelmingly oppose stem cell research. Option C, then, is not adequately supported. US scientists do seem to be turning a blind eye to the potential of adult stem cell research, but we cannot say for certain why. They could be heavily invested in embryonic stem cell research as stated in D, but they could also merely have their hands tied by political policy. As D is not adequately supported, it must be eliminated.
Correct Answer: A

23   We do not, in the first place, know what percentage of the larger population churchgoers represent. In the second place, the majority of US survey churchgoing respondents agree with stem cell research. We have no reason to believe opposition from the churchgoing public is the reason stem cell research is on hold as stated in A. The data is not very specific, but some quick math shows that the majority (about 100%) of survey respondents agree with stem cell research (B). A quick glimpse at the chart also reveals that a significantly lower percentage of the churchgoing population surveyed is against stem cell research (C). Returning to the numbers, it is evident that only about 80% of respondents is neutral (undecided) about stem cell research (D). Clearly the majority 'agrees' with stem cell research as stated in B.
Correct Answer: B

Unit 7

24   The public is calling for post-custodial civil commitment in an effort to permanently cull convicted sex offenders from the general population by locking them up forever. They do not seek to work within the existing legal framework, making sex offences capital crimes subject to the death penalty or life imprisonment, but to apply unprecedented sentencing measures in the form of a post-custodial sentence. This unprecedented approach applies only to sex offenders and does not constitute equality under the law, so option A can be eliminated. Option B, however, applies. The public believes sex crimes can be prevented with civil commitment. Furthermore, we can safely infer that the public believes this is necessary because sex offenders cannot be rehabilitated ('cured'); they will reoffend. The call for post-custodial commitment applies to all sex-offenders, strongly suggesting the public believes that in reality no sex offender can be rehabilitated.   Option C, then, can be eliminated. Civil commitment is controversial and expensive, yet the public demands it. This author points out that the costs are not worth the benefits, but the public, he explains, erroneously believes that civil commitment can protect communities and is, therefore, worth any cost. Clearly D, that communities cannot be kept safe, is not the thinking that underlies the public outcry for post-custodial civil commitment and must be eliminated.
Correct Answer: B

25   The concerns amongst service providers arise not from the fact that most sex offenders can be rehabilitated (A). This may or may not be true, but it is not the principal concern voiced in the passage. Neither do they express concern about possible legal prejudice (B) though the proposed legislation is inherently prejudicial. They do, however, fear that the civil commitment is not cost effective and will ultimately make communities less safe (C). Thinking they have eliminated the problem by locking known perpetrators up forever will result in communities becoming less vigilant, and funds for prevention and detection will likely be used up housing ex-offenders. Civil commitment does amount to an automatic life sentence regardless of the circumstances (D), but this is not the reason those closest to perpetrators and victims are concerned about the proposed legislation.
Correct Answer: C

26   The listing of broad categories of sex crimes in paragraph 2 shows that there is a great deal of disparity in our definitions of sex offenses. The author does not go on to say, however, that some sex crimes are less heinous, meriting differential treatment as suggested in A. Neither does the author elaborate on the mental health aspect of sex offenses (B). The fact that we do not have consensus on what a sex-crime is, as expressed in option C, does suggest that the public is putting the cart before the horse in its call for post-custodial life-long detention of all sex offenders before the term has been adequately and consistently defined. The list of offense categories is extensive, but the author does not include it to show he sympathizes with the public's call for legislation to protect communities (D). Rather the list serves to highlight the disparity in the definition of sex crimes.
Correct Answer: C

27   The passage makes clear that the proposed post-custodial care legislation focuses on

isolating the stranger-type offender who invades communities upon release from prison and then reoffends. Statistically, this hypothetical offender is not the norm. Sex offenders who have completed their sentences, the passage tell us, are less likely to reoffend than any other category of felons. Hence, we have reason to believe that locking them away for life will not significantly reduce the rate of sex offenses. Blanket legislation overlooks the fact that recidivism rates are lowest (B) not highest (A), amongst sex offenders. Option C would actually be an argument in favour of blanket legislation as described in the article. It is not flawed thinking, and C must consequently be eliminated. Option D is a true statement, but like C must be eliminated because is not a flaw in the reasoning underlying civil commitment.
Correct Answer: B

28   D'Amora's statement does not speak to what treatment professionals need to do in the future, but how the operate now; they speak thorough the other groups mentioned. That these other groups are receptive to the message that the majority of sex offenders are rehabilitated under the current custodial-treatment paradigm, suggests that they are in favour of treatment and opposed to blanket civil care legislation being proposed. That being the case, option A can be eliminated. The groups would not be receptive to treatment professionals if they were in favour of the legislation. Similarly, it is safe to say that these are not the groups attacking treatment professionals (B). The groups referred to all have a high level of involvement or expertise and experience. Nothing in the passage suggests that they have not been adequately consulted (C). We can assume, then, that the groups treatment professionals liaise with are opposed to the proposed civil care legislation and are willing to work with treatment professionals to explain that there is a better way to deal with ex-sex offenders (D).
Correct Answer: D

29   The data regarding children (under 18), reveal the minority (about 7%) of children are victimized by strangers – the kind of offender the legislation proposes to lock away forever - while the majority of children are victimized by people they know or are related to. The proposed civil care legislation will not, according to the passage, protect the majority of children from sexual offenses as stated in A. Neither can we say that the proposed legislation will be completely ineffective at protecting communities and victims from sexual predators (B). It will, based on the passage, prevent only a percentage of strangers from reoffending and is likely to have a limited impact. As the proposed civil care legislation will prevent only about 7% of offenses against children at most, option C is supported. As C is a true statement, D must be false. The proposed legislation targets 'strangers' and strangers are not, according to the data, the main victimizers of children.
Correct answer C

30   The combined percentage of persons under 18 victimized by a parent or step parent (A) is about 32%, while the percentage of persons over 18 victimized by a stranger (B) is almost 35%. The total percentage of victims under 18 who were victimized by a non-relative (C) including victims of 'Boy/girl friend (about 4%); Ex-boy/girlfriend (about 1%), Friend/ex-friend (about 22%) Acquaintance/other (about 19%) and Stranger (about 7%) is 53%. The total percentage of persons 18 or older who are victimized by a friend/former friend or an acquaintance is about 50%. As the highest percentage of victims is those under 18 who are victimized by a non-relative the

correct answer here is C.
Correct Answer: C

Unit 8

31	We cannot say from the cartoon that God is uncaring as implied in A; He seems like a busy, frustrated bureaucrat, and bureaucrats may or may not be caring. The cartoon implies that God is too busy to concern Himself with the minor requests of the masses, but this means he is busy, not non-existent, as stated in B. God does, in fact, hear the young man's prayer, and the young man receives an answer. The irony of the cartoon hinges on this. Option C, then, must be eliminated. The young man is referred eventually back to his own heart which tells him to go back to God, creating an endless cycle. The cartoon suggests that our prayers will be answered eventually, but, nothing will come of it. This supports the view put forth in option D, that praying is futile.
Correct Answer: D

32	The young man pictured makes a selfish and rather inane request of God and stays on the line as he is transferred from one 'department' to another. This suggests he is patient, perhaps even committed, not that he is adaptable or malleable (A). His request is foolish in light of his position in the universe and more pressing problems such as global warming and continental shifts that do not bode well for his future, but he is ignorant of this fact. He is fatuous—or inanely foolish. (B). He may be ingénue, artless and innocent, but ingénue also means unworldly; the young man's request sounds very worldly, eliminating option C. The young man is certainly not trenchant, meaning keen, intelligent and penetrating; the inarticulate wording of his request indicates that he is quite the opposite, eliminating option D.
Correct Answer: B

Unit 9

33	Paragraph 1 does not define illnesses, so we have no way of knowing if all illnesses are diseases (A). We can infer, however, that injuries that take long to heal and result in lasting damage can be considered diseases. Option B, then, must be eliminated, and option C is correct. As some injuries are diseases. D, like A must be eliminated simply because paragraph 1 does not define illnesses.
Correct Answer: C

34	Non-specific diseases cannot, the final line of the closing paragraph tells us, be spread from one animal to another. If they are non-communicable, they cannot include viruses (A) which can be spread. As they are non-communicable, they cannot be rarely communicable, and option B must be eliminated. Like all diseases, however, they can be life threatening, so C must be eliminated. Non-specific diseases have a variety of general environmental causes and are non-communicable, meaning that they could include accidents such as giving horses the wrong feed and giving them acute indigestion.

Correct Answer: D

35   Infectious diseases include purely infectious diseases such as hoof and mouth disease that are not transmitted directly, as well as partly infectious diseases that can be transmitted directly or indirectly. Contagious diseases, on the other hand, can only be transmitted directly by means of germs passing from one organism to another. As contagious diseases are transmitted directly, option A is incorrect. As they can only be transmitted directly, option B is also incorrect. Contagious diseases are transmitted by germs and are germ diseases, so option C is incorrect. Infectious diseases include purely infectious diseases that are not contagious and infectious diseases that are contagious, but contagious diseases do not include infectious diseases, meaning that option D is correct.
Correct Answer: D

36   Predisposing causes make an animal more susceptible, but unlike exciting causes which include germs, predisposing causes are not the direct cause of disease. Predisposing causes do not introduce the disease as stated in B, but increase the chances of an animal contracting it. Exciting causes, the author tells us, include germs and a wide range of environmental factors that are difficult to control, but predisposing causes such as drought can be equally difficult to manage. Options C and D, then cannot be correct, as the author does not tell us if predisposing causes are more difficult to control than exciting causes or visa versa. That leaves option A for consideration. Exciting causes include germs and environmental factors that directly introduce disease; that much we know from the passage. We can infer, also, from the description of predisposing causes that they do not make the animal sick directly, but make it more likely to be sick. Option A: predisposing causes are indirect while exciting causes are direct, is supported.
Correct Answer: A

37   Reducing feed and cutting staff would logically result in weakened, predisposed animals and increased likelihood of disease. Options A and B, then, can be eliminated as the animals would have an increased risk of both contagious and infectious diseases, not one or the other. This being the case, option C is correct. Option D can be eliminated as the animals would be predisposed to and more at risk of contracting both infectious and contagious diseases.
Correct Answer: C

Unit 10

38   Although both doctrines would result in profound changes to the existing pro-capitalist social order, it would be inaccurate to say that neither doctrine has principles or basic premise and guidelines. Furthermore, there is no suggestion that either doctrine is lacking in moral scruples—the other meaning of unprincipled. Option A, then, can be eliminated. Option C must also be eliminated as the statements made are consistent with what the passage tells us about Socialism, and its implications for rich and poor. Furthermore, we do not know if Anarchism benefits poorer classes, or if Anarchism is, unlike Socialism, anti-labour (D). Both doctrines, however, 'threaten to wipe out the whole world of those who can afford villas—the propertied and wealthy class. From this we know that both doctrines work against the wealthy and can safely infer that both are anti-capitalist (B).

Correct Answer: B

39   District socialists are novice socialists, the passage tells us, armed with good aims but a very incomplete comprehension of socialism. The author tells us they do some good for the working class and the socialist cause. Hence, they are not useless as stated in A. He does describe district socialists as being middle class and having values governed mainly by their concern for property and respectability. They are, in short, bourgeois. (B) They have a very limited view of the larger ramifications of socialism, so we can also say they are myopic as stated in B. They are ultimately elitists as they truly believe themselves to be part of the governing class, but they are not necessarily hypocritical (C). They do not act contrary of their actual beliefs, but are merely neophytes who cannot yet comprehend the full ramifications of socialism. They are certainly uninformed, but not necessarily misguided as stated in D.
Correct Answer: B

40   The aim of socialism is not model villages, but a total restructuring of society and redistribution of resources; hence A can be eliminated. Administrative socialists, the final paragraph tells us, temper the less administratively experienced working class socialists in their tendency towards anarchism in matters of deportment, suggesting that administrative socialists help working class socialists communicate their needs and achieve their aims. In this sense, they balance the needs of less articulate working class socialists (the have-nots) who have difficulties with control and conduct when speaking about social change, making socialism more palatable to the middle class (the haves) as stated in B. The passage does not speak to administrative socialists promoting socialism in their circles (C), and they do not seek to promote socialism amongst the working class (D) where it is already widely accepted.
Correct Answer: B

41   The author says that the middle class (philanthropic/administrative) socialist personifies the socialist goal of redistributing wealth and doing away with social classes with the picture of a distressed gentlewoman. By so doing they mentally minimize the impacts of social change on the scale proposed by socialism. This does not discredit revolutionary socialists (A) or justify their aims (option B). It is a coping mechanism for middle class Socialists; they have clearly not come to grips with the drastic reforms of working class socialism. This can be interpreted as a criticism of their mentality and commitment (C). The image in question minimizes rather than emphasizes the human costs of revolutionary Socialism (D).
Correct Answer: C

42   A decided advantage of administrative Socialists is that they are masters of control and conduct. They can help the less experienced working class Socialist, who is prone to anarchism, to organize himself administratively. The working class socialist is unruly in comparison to the administrative type Socialist, but the passage does not suggest that that he is disorganized as stated in A. He is less experienced in matters of control and conduct the author tells us, and from his tendency for sentimental anarchism in matters of control and conduct, we can infer that in comparison to his administrative counterpart, the working class Socialist seems inexperienced and overzealous. Option B, then, is supported. Option C must be eliminated as the passage does

not state that working class socialists are well organized or that they lack discipline. Neither does the author suggest, directly or indirectly, that in comparison to administrative Socialists, working class socialists are ineffectual or inarticulate (D). They simply lack training and exposure.
Correct Answer: B

Unit 11

43 That they believe they have the potential to positively influence the lives of foster children does not mean that 73% of those polled are willing to actually help improve foster care (A). The fact that 87% of those polled feel that improving foster care is a priority, is not to say that the remaining 13% (B) believe that it is not. Without seeing the survey form itself, we have no way of knowing if the question had only two possible responses or if 100% of respondents answered the question. 4% (C) represents the difference between the percentage of respondents who feel foster care should be improved and the percentage who have little or no knowledge of foster care. However, there is no logical connection between these numbers and the question, and C must be eliminated because it is random. Option D, however, is supported. If 32% of children in foster care are of African American descent, 68% are not African American. This is a fact supported by the data.
Correct Answer D.

44 The passage is not explicit about the shortcomings of foster care, and the majority of respondents seem vague about the actual deficiencies of the foster care system, so A cannot be correct. Inequalities are noted, but only to make the point that volunteers are needed, meaning B is not correct. No mention of additional government funding for foster care is made, so we can eliminate C. However, the article makes clear that people see the need, have the skills and could make an overwhelming difference as volunteers. The article clearly lobbies for CASA foster care volunteers (D).
Correct Answer: D

45 First of all, candidates must distinguish between the aim and the claims of the article. The aim of the article is to promote volunteerism. The claims of the article are many: that a pool of potentially qualified volunteers is available, that volunteers are needed, and that this perfect match has the potential to improve outcomes for all foster children. Comment I asks if the CASA spokesperson is exaggerating the claim that only 5% children who have volunteers in their lives return to foster care, and addresses claims. Comment IV questions the validity of the data upon which claims are made. How can 83% of people who know little or nothing about foster care tell us anything meaningful about it? It also addresses the article's claims. Comments II and III, on the other hand question the overall advisability of volunteerism, meaning they question the aims of the article. That being the case, only option B can be correct: comments I and IV address the articles claims, while comments II and III address the article's aims.
Correct Answer: B

46 Comment I (A) questions the validity of CASA claims but does not go on to point out how such claims might put young people at risk. Comment II (B), however, demonstrates the risks of

idealistic volunteerism, while Comment III (C) points out that volunteers can be risky to foster children. Comment IV (D) speaks to the weakness of data based on the opinions of people who admittedly know little or nothing about foster care. This kind of data, according to the author, is risky as it gets us all in trouble. Comment IV also exposes a risk associated with foster care. Of the four comments, only Comment I does not expose a risk associated with foster care.
Correct Answer: A

Unit 12

47   The Earth Mother goddess is a metaphor for a utopian state that was quite possibly never achieved amongst her worshippers. There is no indication that she actually lived and reigned on earth or that the 8 tribes were ever at peace. It would be precipitous to say that she actually maintained discipline and social order (A). The goddess had slaves clearly, but this is not to say that her worship was accompanied by slavery (B), and though the slaves die, the story is a myth and there is no suggestion that the religion was accompanied by human sacrifice. The worship of a common goddess possibly connected 8 'otherwise fierce' tribes, but there is no suggestion that a shared religion connects the tribes to a shared (single) ancestry. Ethnology is the study of cultures, particularly in regards to similarities in their historical development. The Earth Mother goddess constitutes a shared characteristic in the 8 different tribes (an unexpected similarity), setting them apart from an ethnologic perspective. It evinces a shared ethnography (D).
Correct Answer: D

48   The Angli considered on their own represent a deviation from what we would expect, and such a difference 'is always suggestive of an ethnological alternative'. This would very significant to the ethnographer, not insignificant as stated in A, but of great importance as stated in B. The ancient Angli and the ancient Venetians share certain characteristics, but there is no suggestion that there is any actual connection between the two. Options C and D can consequently be eliminated.
Correct Answer: B

49   The author makes certain assumptions about island populations based on what we would normally expect. Normally we would expect island populations to derive from the nearest continental population as stated in A. The author does not mention other islands, but nearest continents, so option B, although logical, must be eliminated. Option C is not adequately supported as the author does not tell us if the inhabitants from the nearest continent derive from a single or a diverse gene pool. As we would expect all inhabitants to derive from the nearest continental population, it is unlikely that island populations derive from notably diverse backgrounds as stated in D.
Correct Answer: A

50   Candidates must first invert each of the statements, making them 'untrue', then determine which of the untrue statements has zero impact on the author's premise. If the 8 ancient tribes mentioned did <u>not</u> worship an Earth Mother Goddess, the author's premise would be invalidated, meaning that option A, if not true, would have a substantial impact on the author's premise and must be eliminated. The author compares the Angli with the ancient Venetians (B) simply for

purposes of clarity; his premise does not depend on the comparison, and it would still be true if the Angli were different from the ancient Venetians or if the comparison were omitted altogether. As the statement does not directly support the premise, it cannot undermine the premise, and option B is a correct answer. If the Angli were indeed impacted by diverse foreign elements (C), these elements could have introduced the Earth Mother goddess to them without there being any ethnological connection between the 8 tribes. This would also have a significant negative impact on the author's premise that the 8 tribes are connected ethnographically through the Earth Mother goddess. If the Angli were not an isolated people (D), it is quite possible they would have come to know about the Earth Mother goddess through exposure to tribes other than the 8 tribes mentioned. This would also undermine the author's premise, and D must be eliminated. The only statement which, if untrue, would have no impact on the author's premise is statement A.
Correct answer: A

Unit 13

51   Both the central figure and the data represent inflation; however, they do not depict the same thing. The man is about to 'pop', while the data has 'popped'. According to the data, peek tolerable levels have been reached (A). They are not about to be reached (B). The data tells us nothing at all about the causes, so both options C and D can be eliminated.
Correct Answer: A

52   The cause of inflation (A) is clearly developed in the central figure that presents a demographic type and is clearly suffering from over-consumption. The effects of inflation (B) are developed both in his unhealthy, bulging figure, and in the chart. There we see that the pressure has already caused whatever is being measured to pop. Option C, however, is not developed in the cartoon. The cartoon is satirical in extreme in its obvious criticism of the obvious cause of inflation. It does not, however, speak to solutions for inflationary pressure. The cartoon relies heavily on irony of situation. The central figure's facial expression of wide-eyed surprise tells us that although he is the direct cause of inflation he is clueless as to what's going on. Option D must consequently be eliminated.
Correct answer: C

Unit 14

53   The statement that the primary healthcare system can deal with health problems arising from climate change does not suggest such risks are minimal (A) but that they are preventable (B), as the primary system focuses on prevention. The passage strongly infers that the US has a strong primary healthcare system, but based on the information provided, we cannot tell how much they invest in each level of care. Option C, then, can be eliminated. Similarly, the passage does not speak to the risk climate change posses to individual countries, so we cannot tell which, if any countries, will be most impacted. D, then, must also be eliminated.
Correct Answer: B

54   The evidence provided in the passage, that the claim is no myth because only WHO is authorized to make such a claim, does not tell us if the claim is substantiated by data and actually a fact. We cannot say that the claim is valid simply because WHO made it, and consequently A must be eliminated. Neither, however, can we say it is myth simply because the global focus has not yet shifted to global care as stated in B. Pilot project reports and health statistics, if they had been provided, could likely provide assurance that preventive care works precedent to its being implemented on a global scale. The claim is unsubstantiated, for the reasons stated in C; the evidence provided is extraneous or irrelevant to the claim. We do not know, in the first place, who gave WHO this authority or if this is the author's opinion. Furthermore, no empirical proof is provided to show that the claim is true. Finally, qualifications and authority are no substitute for empirical evidence. That being the case, we cannot say based on the evidence the author provides in the passage that the claim is probably true (D) either.
Correct Answer: C

55   Here candidates must put aside what they may know about the health delivery system and answer the question strictly on the basis of the information provided in the passage. If improving health care by focusing on primary care is the way for developing countries to get out of poverty, we can safely infer that the current focus on providing secondary and tertiary care instead of prevention at the primary level allows preventable diseases to proliferate in developing countries that lack the resources to fund all 3 levels of care. Prioritizing secondary and tertiary care and putting primary care on the back burner, we can say, causes the proliferation of illness which leads to the proliferation of poverty as stated in option D. Option A, sounds logical, but this is not actually stated in or supported by the passage, so it must be eliminated. Options B and C must both be eliminated because the statements are too general to be statements of fact. We do not even know if B and C refer to the overall health system costs or per person costs, so we cannot determine the accuracy of either statement based solely on the passage.
Correct Answer: D

Unit 15

56   Winston Smith, the protagonist, is not grappling within himself (A) or otherwise in an internal conflict regarding his chosen course of action. Therefore, his conflict cannot be described as 'man versus self' (A). He is not in conflict with another individual ('man versus man', B) as no other individual is present. He is, however at odds with his environment (C) which includes the telescreen and the blighted city as well as the ministry where he works and the very flat where he lives. Winston does not reveal himself to be in a universal struggle or to be in conflict with God or other intangible forces that decide our fates as stated in D.
Correct Answer: C

57   At this point, Winston's actions are suspicious (what and why is he hiding from the telescreen?), but he is not overtly defiant. He seems to just be trying to get along in his environment. He lives in depressing conditions, but does not seem particularly depressed (C). Rather, he is focused on whatever it is that has prompted him to forego lunch at the work canteen come home for lunch when food is obviously very scarce. His environment seems dehumanizing,

but we cannot say Winston himself is dehumanized (D). In fact, he seems very human and very vulnerable in his attempt to avoid suspicion. His actions seem premeditated and cautious and are very deliberately (B) executed, making B the best description of the protagonist at this point in the story.
Correct Answer: B

58 To understand Winston Smith's personality type, candidates must determine his underlying motives. He is not motivated by the desire for social interaction, so he is not B, the intrinsic interpersonal type. He does not want public recognition (quite the contrary), so he is not Extrinsic/interpersonal (C). He knows he will receive the utmost punishment in the form of death or forced labour, so there is no question of personal rewards and D can be eliminated. Winston Smith risks all simply to achieve the personal satisfaction of writing in the beautiful, albeit dangerous journal. He is, then, A, the Intrinsic/personal personality type.
Correct Answer: A

59 The central conflict of this story has to do with whether or not Winston will risk death or a 25 year sentence at forced labour just to write a journal. The climax occurs at that point when he actually makes the decision and puts pen to page. Up to that point, when he comes home (A), when he hides in the alcove (B), and when he opens the book (C), he can still turn back. However, the decision is made, the conflict is resolved and the climax is reached in the last line of the passage, when, after a trembling in the bowels that seems prophetic, Winston actually writes the date (D).
Correct Answer: D

60 The passage makes clear that Winston hides away, unseen in the alcove, so option B must be eliminated. It stands to reason that although he cannot be seen when tucked away in the alcove, he can still be heard throughout the flat, eliminating C. We cannot tell for sure if he can see the telescreen or not. We can assume not, but such an assumption is not well supported given that we know very little about the layout or furnishings (i.e. a mirror that would reflect the telescreen). In the meantime, we do know that Winston cannot be seen and we can logically assume he can be heard, meaning that option A is supported.
Correct Answer: A

61 The fact that the telescreen in Winston's flat is placed in an unusual position so a person could hide and write without being detected and that this unusually placed telescreen is in the very flat of man with a strong desire to write is a bone-fide coincidence. Furthermore, it constitutes fair use of coincidence in the passage (A) in that it serves to further the plot but not to resolve the central conflict (will Winston write in the journal or not?). Were the telescreen not in an unusual position, Winston would never have been able to consider writing a journal in the first place. Option B, then, must also be eliminated, as must option C. Even if all the flats had alcoves and blind spots like Winston's (C) this alone would not be significant. It is the unusual and coincidental placement of the telescreen that makes it possible for Winston to hide from the telescreen to write. Option D must be eliminated as the author uses coincidence fairly to further

the action of the story, but not to resolve the central conflict – whether or not Winston Smith will risk his life/freedom to write a journal.
Correct answer: A

Unit 16

62	Data from the Child Fund survey tells us two basic things: that the consumers surveyed are willing to pay more to help end child labour and that they have no idea of the extent of the problem. We cannot safely infer from the data alone that child labour can be abolished globally without hurting labourers, consumers or producers (A). Indeed, consumers even if willing, would be hurt by higher clothing prices. Neither can we tell from the data whether child labour can ever be abolished (B). It is tempting to say that industrialist owners are benefitting most from child labour, but C is barely alluded to in the passage and not addressed by the data. As 55% of respondents were willing to pay higher prices to end child labour, but only 1% knew the actual extent of the problem, we can safely infer that the majority of respondents would be willing to end child labour, and that they are opposed without understanding it. This could be called an emotional reaction and D is supported.
Correct Answer: D

63	The passage speaks predominantly to children engaged in the least prevalent form of child labour; only 7% are involved in manufacturing, including the manufacture of clothing. It does not tell us if this is the most dangerous form of child labour (A), but if only 7% of child labourers would be effected, we can say that paying more for clothing would actually have minimal impact (B) on the numbers and safety of all child labourers. The vast majority would still be out there working in potentially even more dangerous positions. Children fired from their manufacturing jobs would likely have to find work in other fields, so there is no guarantee that these children would enrol and stay in school (C). As they would likely end up working in other fields that are potentially as dangerous as manufacturing and industry, it is likely mortality rates would not reduce, as stated in D.
Correct Answer: B

64	The Child Fund survey shows that a majority of respondents would be willing to pay more to put an end to child labour. It is not, then, safe to say that consumer demand fuels child labour, and Statement I is not supported. Furthermore, although the public surveyed was generally unaware of the extent of child labour, the passage makes clear that poverty, not ignorance, fuels child labour. Educating the public alone will not eradicate poverty, and Statement II is not supported. CEO Goddard, speaking for Child Fund, says that child labour has always and will always exist. She goes on to say that Child Fund is opposed to those forms of child labour that put the child at physical risk or endanger his/her education. Child Fund thus supports some forms of child labour that allow the child to stay in education and Statement III is supported. Poverty, not families, is the root cause of child labour, meaning that Statement IV is not supported. The passage does tell us that universal, compulsory education put an end to child

labour in developed countries. Statement V, then, is supported. As only Statements III and V are supported, C is the correct answer.
Correct Answer: C

Unit 17

65   We see situational irony in the carton in that the scene depicted is the antithesis of what we would expect of an 'open day' tour. Verbal irony is also present in the words of the tour guide who refers to a dead abbot hanging on the wall as a 'jaunty fellow'. Dramatic irony, however, is not at play in the cartoon. Readers are not aware of important information that the characters don't know. As situational and verbal irony are both utilized, we can eliminate options A, B, and C, making D the correct answer.
Correct Answer: D

66   Although abbots are the focus of the cartoon and the guide has a certain monastic appeal, there is nothing tangible such as religious icons to suggest that the scene takes place in a monastery. Option A is possible but weak. On the other hand, the abbots have clearly been killed en masse (slaughtered) and hung like cattle, meaning that option B is supported; the cartoon shows that abattoir is synonymous with slaughterhouse. The term is not used sarcastically (C) or ironically (D) as in both instances there would need to be a second underlying and paradoxical or critical meaning, and neither is present in the larger context of the cartoon. Taken at face value, then, we can safely infer that an abattoir is a slaughterhouse.
Correct answer: B

Unit 18

67   Most people believe that language is declining as civilization declines as though this were a natural and inevitable process outside of human control, and as if language were an entity of its own, or a natural growth (A), and not an instrument or tool used and controlled by humans (B). Language is not causing the decline in society or man, but is declining along with it. Hence we cannot say that most people believe C, that language is the master of man rather than the reverse. This decline in language and civilization cannot, the author tells us, be attributed to a decline in writing (D), but to man's more pervasive underlying attitude about language as something outside his control.
Correct Answer: A

68   The causal relationship described is not humorous, nor does it imitate another's work, so it is not a parody (A). Neither is it a paradox (B), as the relationship described is not self-contradictory, ironic or absurd. Such a causal relationship can, however, be described as a self-fulfilling prophecy. The man who has low self esteem and drinks to cure himself of that feeling is likely to lower his self esteem even more, which is likely to lead to more drinking and more lowering of self esteem, ad infinitum. The relationship serves no one's interests and hence cannot be called a self-serving prophecy (D).
Correct Answer: C

69   The easiest way to unravel the meaning of Example 1 is to start with the relationship between Milton and Shelly. Milton once seemed like Shelly. Furthermore, Milton, not Shelly became increasingly bitter. There is no indication that Milton could not tolerate Shelly (A). Milton became more alien to the founder of the Jesuit sect (B), but it was not the founder but the sect itself (C) that Milton could not be induced to tolerate. Milton's life became increasingly bitter (D), but it was not this that he found intolerable.
Correct Answer: C

70   Candidates will need to isolate the subject of each of the examples to determine which entail criticism, and, if so, what it criticizes. Example 1 does not include criticism. It is a statement, so A can be eliminated. Example 2, however, does use a clichéd idiom (cannot play ducks and drakes) to criticize the use of idioms. Example 3, like Example 1, is expository, not critical and can be eliminated. Example 4 uses sarcasm 'best people' and hyperbolic language ('frantic fascist captains') to criticize opponents of socialism, but does not exemplify the very problem (opponents of socialism) it criticizes.
Correct Answer: B

71   This question is not as difficult as it appears, even if vocabulary isn't your long suit. In each case you have two words to work with. Even if you don't know the meaning of hyperbolic (vastly overstated, rant) raving is better known and it is evident that the authors of several of the comments rant pretty hysterically. Raving is one of our mental vices, so option A can be eliminated. Obtuse, meaning dull, unintelligent, may not be well known, but most of us know meandering means wandering aimlessly. Several of our examples wander from one point to another without ever reaching a conclusion. As they meander unintelligently, B too is one of our vices and must be eliminated. Prudent means wise and conservation can refer to many kinds of economy or holding back. As none of the examples shows a prudent conservation of words or ideas, we can safely say that C is not one of our mental vices and that C is the correct answer. Several of the quotes are garrulous—very wordy, and they do wander around in circles (circumlocution), so D, being one of our vices, must be eliminated.
Correct Answer: C

72   Although Example 4 derives from a communist pamphlet, the subject is socialism; the 'best people', referred to in the opening line represents the middle class or, in other words, the petty-bourgeoisie that opposes and is attacking socialism. That being the case, option A is inaccurate. The fight is against socialism, not communism. Communism, in fact is not mentioned in the body of the example, meaning that B is also inaccurate. The fight is against, not for the socialist revolution, so option C must also be eliminated. The fight mentioned is the fight against socialism as stated in option D.
(D)

Unit 19

73   If the hogs ate table scraps and grain they would be significantly different in terms of their nutrient intake from the women who eat from the table and do not eat grain. Option A, then, certainly does not support the doctor's claim. Option B, however, if true, would support his

claim. It stands to reason that if the two populations had the same diet, and that diet was deficient, they would suffer the same vitamin deficiency. If the hog's diet was adequate (C), this would not support the author's premise. If the hogs were allowed to forage for food, their diet would probably differ significantly from that of the women, meaning that D, if true, would not support the author's premise.
Correct Answer: B

74 The diet utilized on the reservation in question was adequate to meet the nutritional needs of the non-aboriginal population as we see in the statement: 'It should be a matter not only of concern but deep alarm that human beings can degenerate physically so rapidly by the use of a certain type of nutrition, particularly the dietary products used so generally by modern civilization'. We cannot say that government used it intentionally to deprive aboriginal Australians of an adequate diet (A). This is not alluded to in the passage. As the diet was the diet used by 'modern civilization' we cannot say it was nutritionally inadequate for all humans, and option B, then, must be eliminated. That the diet is adequate for the non-aboriginal portion of the population but does not meet the nutritional needs of the aboriginal population means that the dietary needs of the two populations differ as stated in C. The passage does not suggest that native Australians refused the food, thus causing their own nutritional problems, so D can be eliminated.
Correct Answer: C

75 The author's aside about the number of skulls in the collection is unrelated to the topic of paragraph 3, but is included for a reason. He mentions skulls and skeletal remains as if the two were not connected, but this does not in itself indicate the heads were severed (A). It does, however, make readers wonder why so many heads were collected and why they are stored in museums like the remains of extinct species. This does not put colonialism in a good light; it is, in fact, a subtle critique of colonial motives and methods (B). The fact that the number of bones in curation was large does not mean the doctor studied them all or that his study was comprehensive (C). The collecting of human skeletons shows a high degree of disrespect for Aboriginal Australians but does not constitute a racial slur (D).
Correct Answer: B

References

Unit 1: Mysticism and logic. Bertrand Russell. Retrieved from *Project Gutenberg*, http://www.gutenberg.org/catalog/world/readfile?fk_files=774687&pageno=11)

Unit 2: Genetically modified salmon making progress in regulatory review. Retrieved from *Free Content.com*, http://www.copyrightfreecontent.com/technology/genetically-modified-salmon-making-progress-in-regulatory-review/

Unit 3: African Trader by W. H Kingston. Retrieved from *Project Gutenberg*, http://www.gutenberg.org/catalog/world/readfile?fk_files=1524364

Unit 4: How to analyze people on sight Elsie Lincoln Benedict and Ralph Paine Benedict. Retrieved from *Project Gutenberg*, http://www.gutenberg.org/catalog/world/readfile?pageno=1&fk_files=3278048

Unit 5: The smallest woman in the world. Clarice Lispector. Translated by Elizabeth Bishop Retrieved from *Project Gutenberg*, http://www.gutenberg.org/catalog/world/readfile?fk_files=385-920

Unit 6: Cutbacks on care not a solution in economic downturn: avoiding the controversy with adult stem cells. No author, no date. Retrieved from *Copyright Free Content*. http://www.copyrightfreecontent.com/bylined-columns/avoiding-the-controversy-with-adult-stem-cells/

Unit 7: Finding a place for sex offenders: policy makers and advocates differ on where offenders should go when their sentences are up. No author, no date. Retrieved from News USA *Copyright Free Content*. http://www.thefreelibrary.com/Finding+a+place+for+sex+offenders%3a+policy+makers+and+advocates+differ...-a0154178085

Unit 8: Hotline to God. (No author, no date). Retrieved from *Royalty free Cartoons*. http://www.sangrea.net/free-cartoons/relig_hotline-to-god.jpg

Unit 9: *Common Diseases of Farm Animals* R. A. Craig. Retrieved from Project Gutenberg. http://www.gutenberg.org/catalog/world/readfile?fk_files=3164089&pageno=6

Unit 10: Socialism and the Middle Class. H. G. Wells (1929). Retrieved from *Project GutenbergAU*. http://gutenberg.net.au/ebooks13/1303581h.html

Unit 11: Are we tending to our children's garden of hope? (No author, no date) Retrieved from *News USA Copyright Free Content*. http://www.copyrightfreecontent.com/african-americans/are-we-tending-to-our-childrens-garden-of-hope/

Unit 12: R. G. Latham. (No date). The Ethnology of the British Colonies and dependencies. Retrieved from Project GutenbergAU. http://www.gutenberg.org/catalog/world/readfile?fk_files=1530349&pageno=6

Unit 13: Inflationary pressure. Retrieved from *Royalty free Cartoons* http://www.sangrea.net/free-cartoons/social-cartoons.html

Unit 14: Balancing the needs of the many with the benefits of the few. No author, no date. *News USA Copyright Free Content*. Retrieved from www.copyrightfreecoment.com/category/human-interest/social-issues/

Unit 15: George Orwell. *1984*. Retrieved from *Project GutenbergAU*. http://gutenberg.net.au/ebooks01/0100021.txt

Unit 16: Americans would avoid clothes made with child labour. No author, no date. *News USA Copyright Free Content*. Retrieved from www.copyrightfreecontent.com/?s=child+labor

Unit 17: Irony. Retrieved from *Royalty free Cartoons* http://www.sangrea.net/free-cartoons/social-cartoons.html

Unit 18: George Orwell. Politics and the English language. (1946). Retrieved from *Project GutenbergAU* http://gutenberg.net.au/ebooks02/0200151.txt

Unit 19: Weston A. Price *Nutrition and physical degeneration*. 1939 Retrieved from Project GutenbergAU http://gutenberg.net.au/ebooks02/0200251h.html#ch10

Printed in Great Britain
by Amazon